Frommer's®

Portland
day BY day®

1st Edition

by Julian Smith

D0801953

WILEY

John Wiley & Sons, Inc.

Contents

Published by:

John Wiley & Sons, Inc.

111 River St.
Hoboken, NJ 07030-5774

ISBN 978-1-118-06631-7 (paper); 978-1-118-22241-6 (ebk);
978-1-118-24209-4 (ebk); 978-1-118-23631-4 (ebk)

Editor: Alexia Travaglini
Production Editor: Michael Brumitt
Photo Editor: Cherie Cincilla
Cartographer: Andrew Dolan
Production by Wiley Indianapolis Composition Services

Front cover photos: Left: © PCL / Alamy Images. Middle: © Leah Nash.
Right: © Aurora Photos / Alamy Images.
Back cover photo: © Chuck Pefley

For information on our other products and services or to obtain technical
support, please contact our Customer Care Department within the U.S.
at 877/762-2974, outside the U.S. at 317/572-3993 or fax 317/572-4002.

Wiley also publishes its books in a variety of electronic formats. Some
content that appears in print may not be available in electronic formats.

Manufactured in China

5   4   3   2   1

Letter from the Editorial Director

Organizing your time. That's what this guide is all about.

Other guides give you long lists of things to see and do and then expect you to fit the pieces together. The Day by Day guides are different. These guides tell you the best of everything, and then they show you how to see it *in the smartest, most time-efficient way.* Our authors have designed detailed itineraries organized by time, neighborhood, or special interest. And each tour comes with a bulleted map that takes you from stop to stop.

Planning a first-time trip to Portland with the kids? Looking for great ways to explore the Rose City by bike? Or maybe you want to know how to get the most out of the city even on a rainy Pacific Northwestern day. Whatever your interest or schedule, the Day by Days give you the smartest routes to follow. Not only do we take you to the top attractions, hotels, and restaurants, but we also help you access those special moments that locals get to experience—those "finds" that turn tourists into travelers.

The Day by Days are also your top choice if you're looking for one complete guide for all your travel needs. The best hotels and restaurants for every budget, the greatest shopping values, the wildest nightlife—it's all here.

Why should you trust our judgment? Because our authors personally visit each place they write about. They're an independent lot who say what they think and would never include places they wouldn't recommend to their best friends. They're also open to suggestions from readers. If you'd like to contact them, please send your comments our way at feedback@frommers.com, and we'll pass them on.

Enjoy your Day by Day guide—the most helpful travel companion you can buy. And have the trip of a lifetime.

Warm regards,

Kelly Regan, Editorial Director
Frommer's Travel Guides

About the Author

Julian Smith (www.juliansmith.com) writes about travel, science, and just about anything else for many national publications. He's the author of guidebooks to El Salvador, Ecuador, Virginia, and the Southwest, as well as *Crossing the Heart of Africa,* about following the trail of a love-struck British explorer from South Africa to Sudan. Having traveled the world and lived all around the country, he finally picked Portland to settle down with his family.

Advisory & Disclaimer

Travel information can change quickly and unexpectedly, and we strongly advise you to confirm important details locally before traveling, including information on visas, health and safety, traffic and transport, hotels, shopping, and eating out. We also encourage you to stay alert while traveling and to remain aware of your surroundings. Avoid civil disturbances, and keep a close eye on cameras, purses, wallets, and other valuables.

While we have endeavored to ensure that the information contained within this guide is accurate and up-to-date at the time of publication, we make no representations or warranties with respect to the accuracy or completeness of the contents of this work and specifically disclaim all warranties, including without limitation warranties of fitness for a particular purpose. We accept no responsibility or liability for any inaccuracy or errors or omissions, or for any inconvenience, loss, damage, costs, or expenses of any nature whatsoever incurred or suffered by anyone as a result of any advice or information contained in this guide.

The inclusion of a company, organization, or website in this guide as a service provider and/or potential source of further information does not mean that we endorse them or the information they provide. Be aware that information provided through some websites may be unreliable and can change without notice. Neither the publisher nor author shall be liable for any damages arising herefrom.

Star Ratings, Icons & Abbreviations

Every hotel, restaurant, and attraction listing in this guide has been ranked for quality, value, service, amenities, and special features using a star-rating system. Hotels, restaurants, attractions, shopping, and nightlife are rated on a scale of zero stars (recommended) to three stars (exceptional). In addition to the **star-rating system,** we also use a **kids** icon to point out the best bets for families. Within each tour, we recommend cafes, bars, or restaurants where you can take a break. Each of these stops appears in a shaded box marked with a coffee-cup-shaped bullet 🍵.

The following **abbreviations** are used for credit cards:

AE	American Express	DISC	Discover	V	Visa
DC	Diners Club	MC	MasterCard		

Travel Resources at Frommers.com

Frommer's travel resources don't end with this guide. Frommer's website, **www.frommers.com,** has travel information on more than 4,000 destinations. We update features regularly, giving you access to the most current trip-planning information and the best airfare, lodging, and car-rental bargains. You can also listen to podcasts, connect with other Frommers.com members through our active-reader forums, share your travel photos, read blogs from guidebook editors and fellow travelers, and much more.

A Note on Prices

In the "Take a Break" and "Best Bets" sections of this book, we have used a system of dollar signs to show a range of costs for 1 night in a hotel (the price of a double-occupancy room) or the cost of an entree at a restaurant. Use the following table to decipher the dollar signs:

Cost	Hotels	Restaurants
$	under $100	under $10
$$	$100–$200	$10–$20
$$$	$200–$300	$20–$30
$$$$	$300–$400	$30–$40
$$$$$	over $400	over $40

How to Contact Us

In researching this book, we discovered many wonderful places—hotels, restaurants, shops, and more. We're sure you'll find others. Please tell us about them, so we can share the information with your fellow travelers in upcoming editions. If you were disappointed with a recommendation, we'd love to know that, too. Please write to:

Frommer's Portland Day by Day, 1st Edition
John Wiley & Sons, Inc. • 111 River St. • Hoboken, NJ 07030-5774
frommersfeedback@wiley.com

16 Favorite **Moments**

0 — 1/4 mi
0 — 1/4 km

— MAX Light Rail
— Portland Streetcar

NW Nicolai St.
NW York St.
NW Wilson St.
NW 26th Ave
NW Vaughn St.
30
NW Upshur St.
NW Thurman St.
NW Sevier St.
NW 25th Ave
NW 27th Ave
NW Raleigh St.
NW 28th Ave
NW 29th Ave
Wallace
Park
NW Quimby St.
NW Pettygrove St.
NW Cornell Rd
NW Overton St.
NW 22nd Ave
NW Cornell Rd
NW Northrup St.

11 FOREST PARK
NW Marshall St.
NW Lovejoy St.
NW 24th Ave
NW Kearney St.
NW Johnson St.

Macleay
Park
HILLSIDE
NORTHWEST
NW 23rd Ave
NW Westover Rd.
NW Glisan St.

Pittock
Mansion
Acres
W. Burnside St.
NW 21st Ave

SW Park Pl.
SW Park Ave
SW Fairview Blvd.
SW Kingston Ave.
SW Murray St.
SW St. Clair Ave.
SW King Ave.
SW Vista Blvd.
SW Canyon Rd.

SW Fischer Ln.
5 **3**

WASHINGTON
PARK
SW Kingston Dr.
26

SW Fairview Blvd.

1 Browse Powell's City of Books

2 Bike over the Hawthorne Bridge

3 Gaze on Mt. Hood from the International Rose Test Garden

4 Stock up at the Portland State University Saturday Farmer's Market

5 Enjoy a moment of quiet meditation at the Japanese Garden

6 Venture into the Shanghai Tunnels

7 Go to Alberta Street for Last Thursdays

8 People-watch at Stumptown

9 Have lunch at the original food cart "pod"

10 Watch river traffic on the Willamette

11 Ramble through Forest Park

12 Catch a movie at the Bagdad Theater

13 Taste a local pinot noir in the Willamette Valley

14 Go skiing on Mt. Hood

15 Hike to a waterfall in the Columbia Gorge

16 Fly a kite on the beach at Manzanita

Previous page: The "Rose City's" International Rose Test Garden.

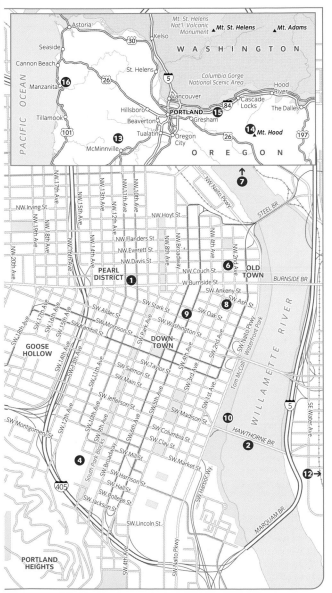

Sometimes Portland seems almost too good to be true. Just try and get locals to stop rhapsodizing about the cuisine, the bike-ability, the mountains and ocean, the beer and wine and coffee and—see what I mean? Once a gritty younger sibling to Seattle, the City of Roses has roared into its own in recent years, becoming a nationwide magnet for creative, outdoorsy types who want a forward-thinking city that's vibrant but manageable. Now Portland swings far above its weight class in everything from coffee roasting to sustainability. Here are just a few of the highlights.

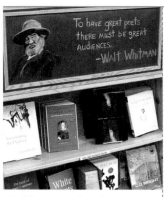

The infamous Powell's bookstore.

❶ Browse Powell's City of Books. The world's top independent bookstore fills an entire city block (and that's just this branch) with over 1.5 million new and used books. It's pure bibliophile nirvana. *See p 10.*

❷ Bike over the Hawthorne Bridge. Bikes are a way of life in Portland, and there's no better way to join the rolling masses than to take a spin across the Hawthorne Bridge over the Willamette River, especially in the evening. *See p 93.*

❸ Gaze on Mt. Hood from the International Rose Test Garden. The flowers are gorgeous, but the views are even better up here in Washington Park; on a clear day you can see multiple snowcapped volcanoes on the eastern horizon, with Mt. Hood at center stage. *See p 13.*

❹ Stock up at the Portland State University Saturday Farmer's Market. Local organic produce, baked goods, food carts, and family-friendly entertainment make the Saturday-morning market at PSU a

Portland State University Saturday farmer's market.

Anything goes on Alberta Street for Last Thursday.

weekend must-do from March through December. *See p 82.*

5 Enjoy a moment of quiet meditation at the Japanese Garden. The most authentic of its kind outside of Japan, Portland's Japanese Garden offers countless serene nooks for contemplating the carefully manicured rocks and greenery—or your own navel. *See p 15.*

6 Venture into the Shanghai Tunnels. Take a guided underground tour for a peek into Portland's sordid past, when drunken sailors and drifters were "Shanghaied"—kidnapped and forced to work on oceangoing ships. *See p 34.*

7 Go to Alberta Street for Last Thursdays. In the rest of the city, it's the first Thursday of every month that brings the gallery openings. Up on Alberta, though, they go with the "Keep Portland Weird" theme and turn the whole street into one big party of art, music, and eccentricity on the *last* Thursday. *See p 24.*

8 People-watch at Stumptown. The quintessential Portland coffee roaster, which recently has gained national recognition, runs a handful of coffee shops that double as primo spots for eyeballing and tattoo-spotting. The downtown branch has the best field of view. *See p 62.*

9 Have lunch at the original food cart "pod" on SW 5th Avenue between Oak and Stark streets, where you can choose from a variety of dishes including Cuban, Thai, Indian, pizza, or "Bulkogi Fusion" (that is, Korean tacos), to name just a few. *See p 109.*

10 Watch river traffic on the Willamette. The Eastbank Esplanade's floating walkway is a great place to spot barges and sailboats. Plus it offers a primo view of the downtown skyline at sunset. *See p 93.*

11 Ramble through Forest Park. Eight square miles of wild forest, streams, gorges, and fern-covered

Portland's backyard: wild and wonderful Forest Park.

The natural beauty of the Columbia Gorge.

hillsides await right on the edge of the city, with more than 70 miles of hiking trails and fire roads to explore. *See p 21*.

⓬ Catch a movie at the Bagdad Theater. Grab a microbrew and a slice of pizza and enjoy a second-run movie in this fully restored 1927 movie palace in the lively Hawthorne District. Stay for dinner or a drink afterward, or venture down

On the Oregon Coast in Manzanita.

the block for dozens of other nightlife options. *See p 41*.

⓭ Taste a local pinot noir in the Willamette Valley. South of Portland, the mild climate and volcanic soil of the Willamette River Valley is ideal for growing wine grapes, which more than 400 wineries take advantage of. *See p 148*.

⓮ Go skiing on Mt. Hood, no matter what the season. It's the only place in the country with lift-accessible skiing year-round. Or just enjoy the views from the 1927 Timberline Lodge, whose snowbound exterior doubled for the hotel in *The Shining*. (The service here is much better, though.) *See p 140*.

⓯ Hike to a waterfall in the Columbia Gorge. There are plenty to choose from, but from the Oneonta Trailhead you can make one easy loop to reach four waterfalls, including a cascade you walk behind. *See p 142*.

⓰ Fly a kite on the beach at Manzanita. The ocean may be too chilly up here to enjoy without a wet suit, but Oregon's coast is as pretty as any on the West Coast, and the charming beach town of Manzanita is within day-trip distance of Portland. *See p 156*. ●

1

The Best **Full-Day Tours**

The Best in **One Day**

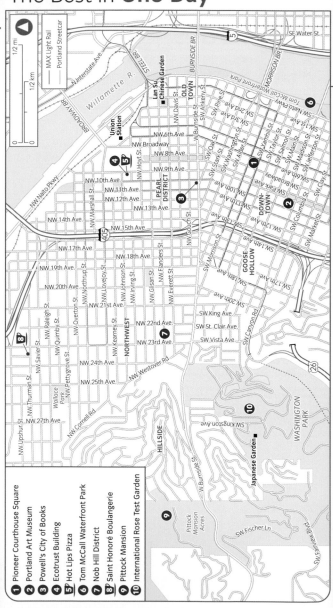

MAX Light Rail
Portland Streetcar

1/2 mi
1/2 km

1 Pioneer Courthouse Square
2 Portland Art Museum
3 Powell's City of Books
4 Ecotrust Building
5 Hot Lips Pizza
6 Tom McCall Waterfront Park
7 Nob Hill District
8 Saint Honoré Boulangerie
9 Pittock Mansion
10 International Rose Test Garden

Previous page: Headquarters of the Ecotrust foundation.

This full-day ramble starts in downtown Portland and ventures up into the West Hills, giving a great overview—literally—of the city's top offerings. After swinging by the riverfront, you'll probably want to trade your walking shoes for a streetcar or bus to reach the final few stops. START: MAX to Pioneer Courthouse/SW 6th Ave. or Pioneer Square South. Bus: 1, 12, 19, or 94 to Pioneer Courthouse Square.

❶ ★ Pioneer Courthouse Square. "Portland's living room" anchors downtown and embodies the Rose City itself in all its eclectic, endearing scruffiness. It's a place to people-watch and mingle, filled with foreign shoppers, local professionals on lunch break, and everyone in between. You'll almost always find some kind of outdoor event going on, be it a farmer's market (Mondays June–Oct), beer festival, jazz concert, or sand castle–building competition. An information center and a TriMet ticket office are available to visitors. ⏱ 30 min. Between SW 6th Ave., Broadway, Yamhill & Morrison sts. ☎ 503/223-1613. www.pioneercourthousesquare.org. Free admission. Daily 5am–midnight. MAX: Pioneer Courthouse/SW 6th Ave. or Pioneer Square South. Bus: 1, 12, 19, or 94.

❷ ★ Portland Art Museum. Founded in 1892, the Northwest's oldest art museum is a one-stop overview of art through history from ancient tribal masks to avant-garde photography. Most works are part of its enviable permanent collection, including more than 5,000 objects by Northwest and Native American artists and a 100-item cache of English silver. Recent acquisitions include a Rembrandt Peale portrait of George Washington and van Gogh's "The Ox-Cart." It's also the home of the Northwest Film Center, which shows classic, foreign, and independent works through the year. ⏱ 1½ hr. 1219 SW Park Ave. ☎ 503/226-2811. www.portlandartmuseum.org. $12 adults, $9 seniors over 54, free for kids under 18, free for everyone 5–8pm the 4th Fri of the month. Tues, Wed & Sat

Pioneer Courthouse Square.

The iconic Powell's Bookstore.

10am–5pm, Thurs–Fri 10am–8pm, Sun noon–5pm. Streetcar: NW 23rd Ave. Bus: 6, 38, 43, 45, 55, 58, 68, 92, or 96 (or 10th Jefferson stop).

❸ ★★★ kids Powell's City of Books. Few cities identify with a bookstore as closely as Portland and Powell's, the world's largest—and many would say best—independent bookseller. Powell's downtown flagship store is a true metropolis of literature, filling a full square block with over 1.5 million books spread through nine color-coded rooms.

Yes, you'll need a map, and probably a cup of coffee from the World Cup coffee shop, but you'll be rewarded with the ultimate bibliophile browsing experience. Powell's buys thousands of used books every day and hosts regular author readings. Don't miss the Rare Books Room, full of signed first editions and an 1814 account of Lewis and Clark's journey worth as much as a modest house. ⏱ *1 hr. 1005 W. Burnside Ave.* ☎ *503/228-4651. www.powells. com. Free admission. Daily*

Ticket Deal

If you plan on making the rounds of the city's major sights, save money with one of four different Portland Attractions Passes. Each is valid for 5 days and available only online at www.travelportland. com. The Big Pass ($53.50 per adult) covers the Portland Art Museum, Lan Su Chinese Garden, Oregon History Museum, Zoo, Pittock Mansion, Children's Museum, Japanese Garden, and World Forestry Center. For more modest itineraries, opt for the separate Washington Park Pass ($31.50), Downtown Pass ($22), or Garden Pass ($18).

9am–11pm; rare book room Sat–Sun 11am–7pm. Streetcar: NW 10th & Couch or NW 11th & Couch. Bus: 20.

4 Ecotrust Building. Technically called the Jean Vollum Natural Capital Center, this brick-and-timber monument to sustainability started as a warehouse in 1895. It was reborn in 2001 as the country's first historic restoration to earn LEED gold certification. Recycled-tire flooring and a water-filtering "eco-roof" are just two of the green techniques incorporated into the redesigned building, which now houses the Ecotrust conservation organization and other enviro-focused businesses and nonprofits. Feel free to wander through the sunny atrium and the Patagonia store, or grab a bite at Hot Lips Pizza (see below). ⏱ *30 min. 721 NW 9th Ave.* ☎ *503/227-6225. www.ecotrust.org/ncc. Free admission. Mon–Fri 7am–6pm. Streetcar: NW 10th Ave. & Irving.*

Grab a thin-crust slice of smoked chicken with mushroom and a bottle of fresh black raspberry soda to enjoy (weather permitting) on the outside patio at **5 Hot Lips Pizza.** Rest assured, the toppings and berries are local and often organic. *NW 10th Ave. & Irving.* ☎ *503/595-2342. $.*

6 ★★ kids **Governor Tom McCall Waterfront Park.** What a different place Portland would be if this 1.5-mile green swath along the west bank of the Willamette River was still a freeway or a seawall, as it was in the past. Instead, it's one of the city's best places to amble, bike, or enjoy one of the many yearly festivals held here. In the hotter months, kids love cooling off in the Salmon Street Springs fountain at Salmon Street, with 185 computer-controlled water jets. More fountains await at the new Saturday Market

The landmark Pittock Mansion.

Waterfront Park on the west bank of the Willamette River.

Pavilion near the Burnside Bridge, just past the 1947 sternwheeler that houses the Oregon Maritime Center and Museum (see p 53). Farther down, the Japanese American Historical Plaza at Davis Street is home to 100 ornamental cherry trees and a "singing" sculpture. 🕐 *1 hr. Packed during festivals. Naito Parkway btw. Steel Bridge & RiverPlace Marina. Free admission. Open daily. MAX: Yamhill District, Oak/SW 1st Ave, or Old Town/Chinatown.*

❼ Nob Hill District. Northwest Portland's strolling commercial district centers on two streets: NW 23rd Avenue, lined with shops and boutiques, and 21st Avenue, with more restaurants. National retailers like Urban Outfitters and Cost Plus World Market cluster at the south end of 23rd near Burnside. Head north for boutiques selling vintage clothes, locally made jewelry, wine, specialty foods, books, and toys. Every block has somewhere to browse, nibble, or rest. 🕐 *1½ hr.*

NW 23rd Ave. btw. Burnside & Thurman sts; NW 21st Ave. btw. Burnside & Northrup sts. Streetcar: NW 23rd & Marshall. Bus: 15.

Named after the patron saint of bakers, the cozy **❽ Saint Honoré Boulangerie** cafe and bakery serves French pastries and rustic breads fresh from the clay firebrick oven. Grab a sidewalk table or a seat at the communal table indoors, both good spots to linger over a cappuccino. *2335 NW Thurman Street (at 23rd Ave.).* ☎ *503/445-4342. $.*

❾ ★★ Pittock Mansion. The home of Portland pioneer Henry Pittock, publisher of the *Oregonian* newspaper and part of the first party to climb Mt. Hood, gazes over the city from 1,000 feet above in the West Hills. Built in 1914, the 23-room mansion combines Northwest materials and workmanship with Turkish, French, and English design touches, along with newfangled inventions like an intercom system and an elevator. The view from the front yard, east across the city, the river, and on to Mt. Hood, is worth the trip in itself—and free. You can hike here along the Wildwood Trail from Washington Park or Forest Park. *3229 NW Pittock Dr.* ☎ *503/823-3623. www.pittock mansion.org. Open 11am–4pm daily, 10am–4pm July & Aug, closed Jan. $8 adults, $7 seniors over 64, $5 kids 6–18.*

⑩ ★★ International Rose Test Garden. Portland's nickname, "The City of Roses," reaches an apogee high in the hills of Washington Park, where about 10,000 rosebushes thrive in the oldest continuously operating official garden of its kind. Founded in 1917, the garden follows its mission to test and preserve new rose hybrids, but even the non-green-thumbed will love the combination of blooms and views, especially in the late afternoon and at sunset. Kiddie-size blooms fill the Miniature Rose Garden, while a wall in the Shakespeare Garden, home to plants mentioned in the Bard's plays, features a fitting quote from *The Two Noble Kinsmen*: "Of all flowers methinks a rose is best." ⊙ *30 min. In summer, go in the evening for smaller crowds. 400 SW Kingston Ave.* ☎ *503/823-3636. www.rosegardenstore.org. Open daily 7:30am–9pm. Free admission. Free guided tours given June–Sept at 11:30am Tues & 1pm Sat & Sun. MAX: Washington Park Station. (In summer, a bus shuttle runs from the station to the gardens every 15 min.) Bus: 63.*

The International Rose Test Garden.

14

The Best in **Two Days**

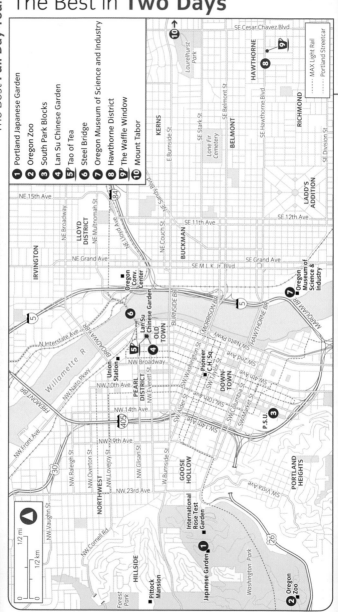

1 Portland Japanese Garden
2 Oregon Zoo
3 South Park Blocks
4 Lan Su Chinese Garden
5 Tao of Tea
6 Steel Bridge
7 Oregon Museum of Science and Industry
8 Hawthorne District
9 The Waffle Window
10 Mount Tabor

········ MAX Light Rail
········ Portland Streetcar

If you have 2 days, start the second in Washington Park, at the first of two outstanding Asian gardens on this itinerary. From there you'll head downhill and across the river (and possibly under it, in the OMSI submarine), ending up in Portland's liveliest southeast district. If you time it right, you'll finish the day with another hilltop sunset, this time from the top of Mt. Tabor. START: MAX Oregon Zoo. Bus 63.

❶ ★★★ **Japanese Garden.** The serene heart of Washington Park encloses five garden styles, a koi pond, and an authentic teahouse with one of the best views of the city and Mount Hood. Considered the finest example of its kind outside of Japan, the 5½-acre garden fits Portland's misty, moody climate perfectly. A walking path winds through meticulously tended landscapes that change with the seasons, from the waterfall and zigzag bridge in the lush strolling pond garden to the carefully raked grooves in the sand and stone garden, perfect for a Zen moment of quiet contemplation. Traditional and seasonal events, including *ikebana* (flower-arranging) exhibits and autumn moon viewing, take place throughout the year. Arrive in the early morning to avoid the crowds. ⏱ *1 hr. 611 SW Kingston Ave.* ☎ *503/ 223-1321. www.japanesegarden. com. Admission $9.50 adults, $7.75 seniors 62 and over, $7.75 college students with ID, $6.50 kids 6–17. Summer noon–7pm Mon, 10am–7pm Tues–Sun; winter noon–4pm Mon, 10am–4pm Tues–Sun. Free guided tours 1 & 2:30pm daily & 10:45am Tues–Sun Apr–Oct; 1pm Sat & Sun Nov–Mar. MAX: Washington Park; free bus shuttle to garden in summer. Bus: 63 on weekdays only.*

❷ ★★ kids **Oregon Zoo.** Started in the 1880s by a downtown druggist who collected animals from friendly sailors, Oregon's premier zoo is now home to more than 2,000 animals, including many threatened and endangered species. Start with the black bears, cougars, and wolves of the Pacific Northwest; then venture into an Amazon flooded forest, eyeball a Serengeti cheetah, or come nose-to-snout with a linebacker-size orangutan. They're particularly proud of their Asian Elephant breeding program, whose ranks include local celebrity Packy and baby Sam, born in 2008. Hop aboard a ⅝-scale train pulled by a real steam engine around the zoo or on a 4-mile loop to the Rose Test Garden and Japanese Gardens. From June to August, the zoo hosts open-air concerts on summer evenings with local and national acts. ⏱ *1½ hr. Animals are most active in early morning & late*

The Oregon Zoo.

The Oregon Museum of Science and Industry (OMSI).

afternoon. 4001 SW Canyon Rd. ☎ 503/226-1561. www.oregonzoo. org. Admission $10.50 adults, $9 seniors over 64, $7.50 kids 3–11, $4 per person the 2nd Tues of every month, show MAX ticket for $1.50 discount. Summer 9am–6pm, grounds open until 7pm; fall–spring 9am–4pm, grounds until 5pm. MAX: Washington Park. Bus: 63 on weekdays only.

South Park Blocks, downtown Portland.

❸ **South Park Blocks.** Portland's first parks, set aside in 1852, are still a peaceful respite from the hubbub of downtown. Stately oaks, elms, and maples shade 12 grassy blocks between SW Salmon and SW Jackson streets. Public art on every block ranges from the classical (statues of Teddy Roosevelt and Lincoln) to the abstract (three granite blocks titled "Peace Chant"). The southern end, part of Portland State University, is closed to car traffic and home to the Portland Farmer's Market (see p 82) on Saturday mornings from spring through fall. ⏱ *30 min. Open daily 5am–9pm.*

❹ ★★ **Lan Su Chinese Garden.** Always a surprise amid the general shabbiness of what's left of Chinatown, this hidden gem is a fully authentic Ming Dynasty–style garden complete with lake, bridges, and a two-story teahouse pavilion. All the wooden buildings, decorative windows, and 500 tons of rock were shipped in from Suzhou, China, as were the workers who assembled them. Every season highlights the carefully planned landscape and plantings in a different way, from spring blooms and fall leaves to the bare branches of winter. ⏱ *45 min. Entrance at NW 3rd Ave & Everett*

Travel Tip

Don't worry about a ticket if you're traveling by MAX or street-car in the heart of Portland. TriMet's Free Rail Zone covers MAX stations in most of downtown and as far as the Lloyd Center, and the streetcar from NW Irving to SW River Drive. Just look for the Free Rail Zone logos at the station.

St. www.lansugarden.org. Admission $8.50 adults, $7.50 seniors 62 and over, $6.50 students with ID & kids 6–18. Free tours daily at noon & 1pm. Open daily, summer 10am–6pm; winter 10am–5pm. MAX: Old Town Chinatown. Bus: 4, 8, 9, 16, 35, 44, or 77.

What better way to recharge than over a cup of oolong at **5 Tao of Tea Teahouse** inside the Tower of Cosmic Reflections, gazing over Lake Zither? Along with a huge selection of teas, they offer a short list of sweets and nibbles. ☎ 503/224-8455. $.

6 Steel Bridge. Of all Portland's bridges, this 210-foot span, built in 1912, offers the most ways to cross the Willamette River. The upper deck carries cars and MAX light rail, while the lower accommodates trains, cyclists, and pedestrians; the latter two on a cantilevered walkway on the southern side that connects Waterfront Park to the Eastbank Esplanade. Bridge buffs ahoy: It's the world's only double-deck vertical lift bridge whose lower deck can lift independently of the upper one, and it's the second-oldest vertical lift bridge in North America. (Hawthorne Bridge—also in Portland—is the oldest.) ⏱ 15 min. Btw. NW

Culture, history, and nature at Lan Su Chinese Garden.

The USS Blueback *submarine at OMSI.*

Naito Pkwy./NW Glisan St. & N Interstate Ave./NE Multnomah St.

7 ★ kids **Oregon Museum of
Science and Industry.** Set, fittingly, in a former power plant on
the east bank of the Willamette
River, OMSI celebrates knowledge
and technology in all forms. Hands-
on exhibits demonstrate everything
from aging to nanotechnology,
including a replica of the Gemini
space capsule and a chemistry lab

The Vera Katz Eastbank Esplanade.

for mixing concoctions (safely). If
that's not enough, catch a show in
the Omnimax theater or the largest
planetarium in the Northwest, or
head out to the river to tour the
210-foot USS *Blueback*, the country's last diesel submarine. Adults
can avoid the near-constant crowds
of schoolchildren by coming for
"OMSI After Dark" evening events,
open only to the 21-and-over crowd.
⏱ *1 hr. 1945 SE Water Ave.*
☎ *503/797-4000. www.omsi.edu.
Tues–Sun 9:30am–5:30pm. Admission $12 adults, $9 seniors over 62 &
kids 3–13, $2 per person the 1st Sun
of every month. Submarine, planetarium & Omnimax tickets are extra,
& various combination deals are
available. Bus: 4, 6, 10, 14, 31, 32,
or 33.*

8 **Hawthorne District.** Portland's eclectic epicenter stretches
along Hawthorne Boulevard
between 30th and 42nd avenues,
packed with restaurants, cafes,
bars, boutiques, thrift stores, and
theaters. Most of the action is concentrated between 34th and 39th

Biking Mount Tabor.

avenues, including the historic Bagdad Theater & Pub (see p 41) and a branch of Powell's Books. It's an easily walkable stretch, with plenty of options for shopping and noshing. *Bus: 14.*

If you still think waffles are just for breakfast, peek around the corner from the Bread and Ink Café for **9 The Waffle Window**'s bright blue doorway serving creative concoctions like the Three Bs (brie, basil, and pepper bacon). They also offer classic waffle toppings like berries, jam, and syrup. Sit outside at the picnic tables or inside on rainy days. *3610 SE Hawthorne Blvd.* ☎ *503/239-4756. $.*

10 Mount Tabor. How many cities in the continental U.S. can boast an extinct volcano within their boundaries? Only two, actually: Bend and Portland, whose volcanic heritage looms in the form of this 630-foot cinder cone. It's topped by three reservoirs and a 190-acre city park featuring forests laced with trails for bikers and hikers. Near a large playground is an amphitheater where free outdoor concerts

happen on Tuesday evenings in the summer. *Open daily 5am–10pm, closed to motor vehicles Wed. Enter at SE Salmon St. & 60th Ave., SE Lincoln & 64th Ave., SE Yamhill & 69th Ave., or SE Harrison St. & 71st Ave. Bus: 4, 15, or 71.*

Tai chi, Lan Su Chinese Garden.

The Best in **Three Days**

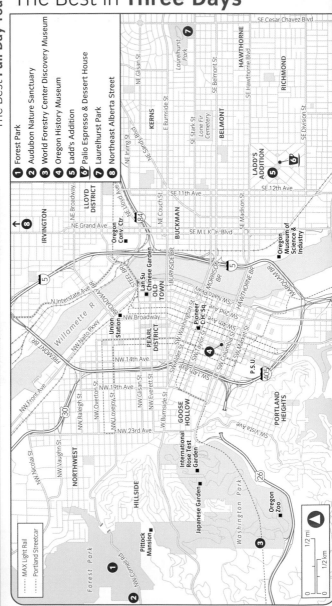

1 Forest Park
2 Audubon Nature Sanctuary
3 World Forestry Center Discovery Museum
4 Oregon History Museum
5 Ladd's Addition
6 Palio Espresso & Dessert House
7 Laurelhurst Park
8 Northeast Alberta Street

MAX Light Rail
Portland Streetcar

1/2 mi
1/2 km

Having 3 days to play with lets you venture farther afield; in this case, into the offbeat, artsy northeast section of town. Plus you'll have time to explore a few of Portland's outdoor options in more depth, including one of the largest urban parks in the country.

START: **Bus 15 to NW Thurman & 29th Ave. (Lower MacLeay Park).**

1 ★★ **Forest Park.** Portland's leafy backyard covers 8 square miles of the West Hills, making it the country's largest urban forest reserve. (It's over six times the size of New York's Central Park.) It's still home to most of the species that were here when William Clark visited on a side trip in 1806—from bobcats and black-tailed deer to pygmy owls and woodpeckers. Small streams and over 70 miles of trails lace the forested hillsides and valleys, including the popular 30-mile Wildwood Trail, a National Recreation Trail. (Mountain bikers are limited to access roads and fire lanes.) It's also amazingly close to downtown; the Lower MacLeay Park trail head at the end of NW Upshur Street is probably the easiest to access on foot, and NW Thurman Street turns into Leif Ericson Drive, the park's main travel artery. From

there you can hike to the Pittock Mansion, Washington Park, or as far as Gresham on the 40-Mile Loop from the Wildwood Trail (p 87). 🕐 *1½ hr. Numerous trail heads.* ☎ *503/823-7529. www.forestpark conservancy.org. Free admission; open daily. Dogs must be leashed. Bus: 15.*

2 kids ★ **Audubon Nature Sanctuary.** For a quick taste of Portland's lush city-edge forests, with a close-up animal encounter or two thrown in for free, head to this 150-acre public reserve at Forest Park's southern end. Four miles of trails lead along Balch Creek and under old-growth Douglas firs, and from here you can access the Wildwood and Upper MacLeay trails in Forest Park proper. The Wildlife Care Center is Oregon's oldest and most

Hiking in Forest Park.

Audubon Nature Sanctuary.

active, giving thousands of injured animals another chance at life in the wild every year. You never know who'll be in residence: Beavers, bald eagles, great horned owls, and turtles have all made appearances.

The Forest in Focus exhibit at the Discovery Museum.

🕐 *1 hr. 5151 NW Cornell Rd.* ☎ *503/ 292-6855. www.audubonportland. org/sanctuaries. Open daily, trails dawn to dusk, care center 9am–5pm. Free admission. Bus: 15 (plus 1.5-mi. walk from NW 23rd & Lovejoy St.).*

3 **kids** **World Forestry Center Discovery Museum.** Timber is a cornerstone of Northwest history, and this small hands-on museum in Washington Park shows how important forests are to the region's past and future. Treading the sometimes-delicate line between environmental stewardship and timber extraction, it has two floors of interactive displays that range from virtual tours through the world's major kinds of forest to a timberjack harvester simulator. 🕐 *1 hr. 4033 SW Canyon Rd.* ☎ *503/228-1367. www.world forestry.org. Admission $8 adults, $7 seniors 62 and over, $5 children 3–18. 1st Wed of each month $3 per person. Open daily 10am–5pm. MAX: Washington Park. Bus: 63.*

4 **Oregon History Museum.** Delve into the past of Oregon and the entire Pacific Northwest at this collection, run by the Oregon Historical Society on the South Park Blocks. The main permanent exhibit is the award-winning "Oregon My Oregon," which takes up an entire floor and includes a 9,000-year-old sagebrush sandal and the lunch counter from Newberry's, a famous downtown eatery. Other exhibits, permanent and traveling, cover topics such as Lewis and Clark, the Oregon Trail, western Native baskets, and Portland's new Major League Soccer team, the Timbers. ⏲ *30 min. 1200 SW Park Ave.* ☎ *503/306-5198. www.ohs.org. Admission $11; students over 18 & seniors over 60 $9, children 6–18 $5. Tues–Sat 10am–5pm; Sun noon–5pm. MAX: SW 6th & Madison sts. Streetcar: Art Museum. Bus: 6, 38, 43, 45, 55, 58, 68, 92, or 96.*

❺ ★ Ladd's Addition. One of Portland's oldest residential districts breaks up the east side's neat road grid with an eight-by-ten-block of diagonals and roundabouts, inspired by Pierre L'Enfant's spider-webby plan for Washington, D.C. Named after William Ladd, a 19th-century mayor who had a farm here, Ladd's is a designated historic district that's great for a shady walk under the old elm trees that line the streets. The neighborhood's odd road alignments leave room for four diamond-shaped gardens, each overflowing with roses (of course) in season, as well as a larger circular park inside the central roundabout. ⏲ *45 min. Btw. SE Hawthorne St., Division St, 12th Ave. & 20th Ave. Bus: 4, 10, 14, or 70.*

Rest your feet and enjoy a Mexican Mocha or a slice of key lime pie at **❻ Palio Espresso & Dessert House,** a cozy coffee shop and cafe right across the street from the neighborhood's central park garden. Stumptown coffee and plenty of different teas are served in a setting that feels a bit like an antique bookstore. *1996 SE Ladd Ave.* ☎ *503/232-9412. $.*

The River Raft Adventure at Discovery Museum.

Please Turn Around
And Face The Monitor

PDX Playlist

Seattle and L.A. may get more press, but Portland has been home to outstanding live music ever since The Kingsmen garbled their way through "Louie, Louie" in one take in 1963. (After a 2-year obscenity investigation, the FBI concluded the song was "unintelligible at any speed.") Here's the perfect soundtrack of local, or at least once-local, artists for your visit.

- "Louie, Louie," The Kingsmen, 1963
- "I Can't Wait," Nu Shooz, *Poolside*, 1986
- "Ride," Dandy Warhols, *Dandys Rule, Ok?* 1995
- "I Will Buy You A New Life," Everclear, *So Much For the Afterglow*, 1997
- "Between the Bars," Elliott Smith, *Either/Or*, 1997
- "Light Rail Coyote," Sleater-Kinney, *One Beat*, 2002
- "Phantom Limb," The Shins, *Chutes Too Narrow*, 2003
- "Let's Never Stop Falling in Love," Pink Martini, *Hang On Little Tomato*, 2004
- "On The Bus Mall," The Decemberists, *Picaresque*, 2005
- "People Say," Portugal, The Man, *The Satanic Satanist*, 2009

❼ ★ kids Laurelhurst Park.
Thank former mayor William Ladd (see Ladd's Addition, above) for this 26-acre park in the neighborhood of the same name (Laurelhurst). Grand old trees shade paved trails, picnic tables, and open lawns, including an off-leash area for dogs; it is most definitely one of the city's prettiest parks. Originally a spring-fed pond, 3-acre Firwood Lake was dredged in 2011 and fitted with a water circulation and aeration system. The lawn next to it is the best spot on the east side to lounge away a sunny Friday afternoon. A smaller "play park" section between SE Oak and Stark streets has tennis courts, a soccer field, a playground, bathrooms, and a small dance studio for public recreation classes. ⏲ *30 min.*

Btw. SE 33rd & 39th aves., Oak & Ankeny sts. Open daily 5am–10:30pm. Bus: 75.

❽ ★ Northeast Alberta Street. Sure, it's a case study in gentrification with a high hipster factor, but Northeast Alberta Street between 15th and 33rd avenues is still one of the more interesting districts on Portland's east side, and the perfect place to end your day. The main drag is chock-full of restaurants, shops, theaters, and art galleries. Most businesses throw their doors open on the last Thursday of every month for the city's funkiest monthly street fair, complete with music, clowns, and carefully balanced "tall bikes." ⏲ *1 hr. NE Alberta St. btw. 15th & 33rd aves.* ●

Portland **with Kids**

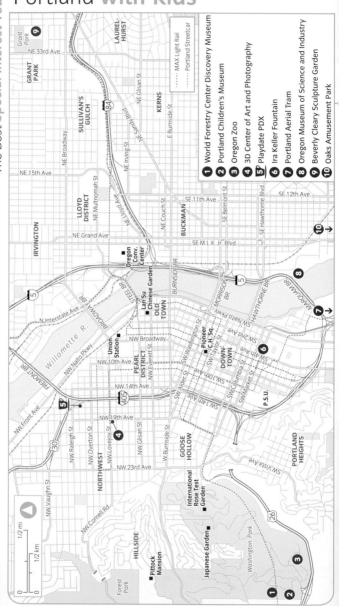

---- MAX Light Rail

········· Portland Streetcar

1 World Forestry Center Discovery Museum
2 Portland Children's Museum
3 Oregon Zoo
4 3D Center of Art and Photography
5 Playdate PDX
6 Ira Keller Fountain
7 Portland Aerial Tram
8 Oregon Museum of Science and Industry
9 Beverly Cleary Sculpture Garden
10 Oaks Amusement Park

Previous page: Cooling off at the Salmon Street Springs fountain.

Portland repeatedly gets voted one of the best cities in the country to raise kids. Certain neighborhoods, especially on the east side, are full of young couples with children, and strollers and baby backpacks seem almost as ubiquitous as bikes in parks and on sidewalks. Kids love the bridges, trails, and rivers, and there are plenty of activities right in town to keep them busy, including the sites adjacent to each other in Washington Park. START: MAX to Washington Park. Bus 63 on weekdays.

1 World Forestry Center Discovery Museum. At this paean to all things arboreal, kids especially love the virtual smoke-jumper and river-rafting exhibits—and after a visit here they'll be ready to dive into the real forests of Washington Park right outside. See p 22, **3**.

2 ★★ Portland Children's Museum. Right next door is a castle of creativity and fun, one of the oldest of its kind in the country. The displays are constantly updated—and hands-on, of course, including exhibits themed around popular characters like Curious George and Clifford the Big Red Dog. Kids age 10 and under can burrow in the rubber gravel of the Dig Pit, sculpt a city in

the Clay Studio, build something in the Garage, or take the stage at the Play It Again Theater. A stop at the Water Works will probably require a change of clothes, but it's worth it. The Baby's Garden caters to tots under 3. A varying schedule of classes and story times keeps things fresh. ⏱ *1½ hr. It can get crowded & chaotic at peak times, so consider coming on weekdays & later in the afternoon, after the school groups have left. 4015 SW Canyon Rd.* ☎ *503/223-6500. www.portlandcm. org. Open daily 9am–5pm, Thurs 9am–8pm, free 1st Friday of every month 4–8pm. Admission $9 age 1–54, $8 over 54, free under 1. MAX: Washington Park. Bus: 63 on week-days only.*

Budding chefs at the Portland Children's Museum.

The Oregon Zoo.

③ ★★ Oregon Zoo. It's hard to decide which animals children like best here: the frolicking river otters, the powerful Amur tigers, or the acrobatic chimpanzees. In any case, the miniature train is a sure-fire favorite, circling the zoo and venturing off into the rest of Washington Park. Come early or stay late to increase your odds of seeing animals in action. *See p 15, ②*.

④ 3D Center of Art and Photography. Whatever this quirky downtown collection lacks in size it more than makes up for in depth—illusory though it may be. This collection of 3-D images, both still and moving, ranges from stereocards from the Civil War to View-Master viewers (started here in 1939) to today's 3-D cameras. Interactive displays explain how the illusion of three-dimensionality is created, and a theater shows experimental films in the back. (New exhibits and films often open on first Thurs) The gift shop alone is worth a visit. ⏲ *30 min. 1928 NW Lovejoy St.* ☎ *503/227-6667. www.3dcenter.us. Admission $5, 14 and under free. Free 1st Thurs of every month 6–9 pm; Thurs–Sat 11am–5pm; Sun 1–5pm. Streetcar: NW Lovejoy & 18th. Bus: 77.*

At **⑤ Playdate PDX**'s 7,500-square foot indoor playground, you can enjoy a panini and coffee (or glass of wine) while your progeny runs wild on a multistory castle with ropes, swings, and slides. Admission isn't cheap—$8 to $10 per kid, $4 to $5 age 3 and under—and it can get packed; but on a rainy day, nothing relieves stress better than a room full of Nerf guns to shoot at each other. *1434 NW 17th Ave.* ☎ *503/227-7529. www.playdatepdx.com. $.*

3D Center of Art and Photography.

Outdoor Fountains

In the heat of the summer, the irony of cavorting in water in such a damp city evaporates like puddles on concrete, and kids pack Portland's many public water fountains. Even if it's too cool or cloudy to splash, they're still fun to see. Just don't take a drink; they all use chlorinated, recycled water.

Jamison Square Fountain. One of Portland's most popular hot-weather destinations fills half a block in the Pearl District. The shallow wading pool is geared toward toddlers and babies, while older kids can clamber up the steps of the cascades. The other half of the park consists of grass and trees for lounging in the shade. *NW 11th Ave. & Johnson St.*

Bill Naito Legacy Fountain. Actually two fountains at one end of the new Portland Saturday Market plaza, this consists of a small amphitheater with a series of water arches and a flat plaza under a glass roof with dozens of vertical jet "blowholes." The latter is turned off and filled with vendors during the market. *SW Naito Pkwy. & SW Ankeny St., in Governor Tom McCall Waterfront Park.*

Salmon Street Springs. The most distinctive and impressive of the city's fountains anchors the southern end of Governor Tom McCall Waterfront Park. Concentric circles of 185 jets spout water in every imaginable pattern, controlled by an underground computer that changes the pattern every 20 minutes. Almost 5,000 gallons of water a minute gush at peak volume— so older toddlers, grade-schoolers, and pre-teens will enjoy it most. *SW Naito Pkwy. & SW Salmon St. in Governor Tom McCall Waterfront Park.*

Teachers Fountain. The newest public square downtown, dedicated to educators, has a gentle fountain with low jets and burbles feeding into a shallow pool ringed by benches. *SW Yamhill & SW Park aves.*

6 Ira Keller Fountain. If you can't make it up the Columbia Gorge, this is the closest you'll come to a waterfall downtown: an abstract of edges and drop-offs holding 75,000 gallons of water. Too steep and slippery for climbing, this fountain is more for watching and wading. 🕐 *1 hr. SW 3rd Ave. & SW Clay St. Fountains generally flow from spring through fall.*

7 Portland Aerial Tram. A fun trip to the hospital? Yes, when it involves a ride in a space-age pod that sails ⅔ of a mile (and 500 feet up) from Oregon Health Science University's Center for Health & Healing at South Waterfront to the main OHSU campus up on Marquam Hill. On nice days, the $57-million tram offers views of Mt. Hood, Mt. St. Helens, and, of course, the river and

The Portland Aerial Tram.

downtown. 🕐 *30 min. Departs every 6–10 min. Lower terminal and ticket kiosk at 3303 SW Bond Ave. www.portlandtram.org. Admission $4 round-trip, children 6 and under free. Mon–Fri 5:30am–9:30pm; Sat*

9am–5pm; Sun 1–5pm. Streetcar: OHSU Commons. Bus: 35 or 36.

❽ ★ Oregon Museum of Science and Industry. From the Omnimax dome theater to the real-live submarine, the earthquake simulator to the pint-size science playroom upstairs for kids 6 and under, OMSI is 219,000 square feet of interactive learning and educational fun. *See p 18, ❼.*

❾ Beverly Cleary Sculpture Garden. Fans of the famous children's author will find statues of three of her most beloved characters—Henry Huggins, Ramona Quimby, and Henry's dog, Ribsy—in Grant Park, which appears in several of her books. The statues are just south of the playground near Grant High School, which Cleary also wrote about. Across 33rd Street, the grade school she attended as a child now bears her name. (In the public library branch at NE Tillamook and 40th Ave., a large map of the neighborhood marks more local landmarks in her

Beverly Cleary Sculpture Garden.

Oaks Amusement Park.

books.) ⏱ *15 min. NE Brazee St. &
NE 33rd Ave. Bus: 73.*

⑩ ★★ Oaks Amusement Park.
A time warp on the bank of the Willamette River near Sellwood, Oaks
Amusement Park was inaugurated
in 1905 to accompany the Lewis and
Clark Centennial Exposition. The oldest continually operating amusement park in the country, it has two
dozen modern rides, including the
Scream-n-Eagle and the Looping
Thunder Roller Coaster, along
with classics like a Ferris wheel,
a Tilt-a-Whirl, and a miniature train
that chugs along the waterfront.
Nostalgists like the 1912 carved
carousel, midway games, and

wooden skating rink with a suspended pipe organ. It's free to enter
and use the picnic grounds, where
a path leads down the bluff to the
river's edge. ⏱ *2 hr. 7805 SE Oaks
Park Way.* ☎ *503/233-5777. www.
oakspark.com. Hours vary; rides
usually Mar–Oct Sat & Sun noon–
7pm; June–Aug Tues–Sun noon–9pm,
skating rink Tues–Sun in afternoon
and evening sessions year-round.
Admission to grounds is free, ride
tickets $2.25 each, unlimited ride
bracelets $11.75–$14.75, go-karts
$5 driver, $2 passengers, skating
$5.75–$6.75, skate rental $1.50–$5.
Bus: 70.*

Offbeat Portland

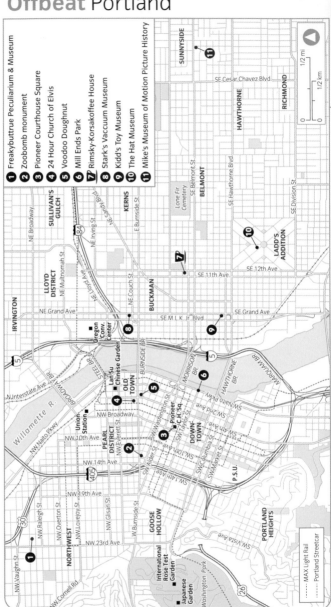

1 Freakybuttrue Peculiarium & Museum
2 Zoobomb monument
3 Pioneer Courthouse Square
4 24 Hour Church of Elvis
5 Voodoo Doughnut
6 Mill Ends Park
7 Rimsky-Korsakoffee House
8 Stark's Vaccuum Museum
9 Kidd's Toy Museum
10 The Hat Museum
11 Mike's Museum of Motion Picture History

MAX Light Rail
Portland Streetcar

1/2 mi
1/2 km

"Keep Portland Weird" isn't just a ubiquitous local bumper sticker; here it's a way of life. Whether it's the long cloudy winters or the concentration of creative types (or both), Portland has a streak of strange it wears proudly. The "Velveteria" velvet painting museum may have moved on to sunnier climes, but there's plenty more here to amuse your inner oddball, from one-of-a-kind museums to kooky and chaotic annual events. START: **Bus 17 to NW Thurman Ave. & 22nd Pl.**

① ★ Freakybuttrue Peculiarium & Museum. Part museum, part art gallery, part gift shop, and part ice-cream parlor, the Peculiarium lives up to its name. Here you'll find skulls, vampire-killing kits, and a 10-foot Sasquatch, just for starters. There's an interactive Alien Autopsy and a motel room painted entirely in glow-in-the-dark paint, and changing exhibits on things like spontaneous human combustion. The in-house magician gives lessons and live shows on Friday evenings. Finish off your visit with something from the ice-cream bar, but be warned: The Bug-Eater's Delight is not a descriptive metaphor. 🕐 *30 min. 2234 NW Thurman St.* ☎ *503/227-3164. www.peculiarium.com. Free admission. Open Thurs–Sun 11am-9pm. Magic shows Fri 8pm. Bus: 17.*

② Zoobomb monument. One of the proudest and definitely most unusual traditions in this bike-mad city is the weekly Sunday evening ride—and I use the term loosely—from the zoo down the West Hills. It's the strangest peloton you've ever seen, full of tall bikes, kids' bikes (ridden by adults), skateboards, and essentially anything wheeled and human-powered. Some riders dress in outlandish costumes, and everyone has a blast. If you don't have your own bike, don't worry: outside the American Apparel store at 13th Avenue and West Burnside Street is a monument (read: pile on a pole) of bikes, including some

spares, chained up and waiting for Sunday night. A gold-plated minibike tops the public artwork, also known as the "People's Bike Library of Portland." 🕐 *15 min. 13th St. & West Burnside Ave. Zoobomb riders meet here every Sun around 8:30pm. Bring a bike if you have one, helmet, MAX fare, and lights. www.zoobomb.net. Bus: 20.*

③ kids ★ Pioneer Courthouse Square. The most trafficked block in the city still has a few tricks up its sleeves. Throughout the plaza are bricks engraved with the names of

Weird but true: the Zoobomb monument.

Legal graffiti, Pioneer Courthouse Square.

donors who helped fund the space—or pseudonyms. See if you can find Mr. Spock, Sherlock Holmes, Jesus Christ, and Bilbo Baggins. (You can order your own for $100.) The small amphitheater in the northwest corner, below the bronze chessboards, is an echo chamber; if you stand on the central marble stone and speak, it creates a huge echo that only you can hear. Next to the amphitheater is a pole-mounted weather machine. A series of lights show the temperature, and every day at noon, a fanfare announces the weather prediction, indicated by an icon that pops out of the globe on top: a heron for light rain, a dragon for heavy rain, and a sun for, well, sun. On the 6th Avenue side of the plaza, a milepost indicates the distance to places like Mt. Hood, Moscow, Timbuktu, and Tipperary ("a long way"). *See p 9,* ❶.

Shanghai Tunnels

In the late 19th century, Portland was the second biggest port on the West Coast, and miles of underground tunnels were built to move goods from the riverside docks into the city. They were also used to kidnap thousands of drunks and transients from bars, brothels, and boardinghouses to press into service on large sailing ships. Hired thugs used opium knockout drops and trapdoors to grab their prey, receiving payment for each warm body they delivered. At its peak, Portland was said to lead the world in the practice, called *Shanghaiing* since victims often woke up at sea on ships headed to Asia. The tunnels were sealed in 1941, but you can tour them today with Portland Walking Tours (☎ **503/774-4522,** www.portland walkingtours.com). Tours meet outside Old Town Pizza at 226 NW Davis St. at 2pm daily Apr–Nov, Dec–Mar Fri–Sat, for $19 adults, $15 seniors 65 and older and youth 11–17, $5 children 5–10).

4 24-Hour Church of Elvis. A miniature coin-operated art gallery installed on the outside of a Chinatown storefront may not be your idea of a "church," but when you're talking Elvis, all bets are off. Local artist Stephanie "Stevie" Pierce designed this cute, kitschy sidewalk shrine that offers fortunes, bicycling Barbie dolls, "Elvis detectors," and even fully legal weddings (by appointment). ⏱ *15 min. 408 NW Couch St. www.24hourchurchofelvis. com. Open daily 24 hr. MAX: NW 5th & Couch. Bus: 9, 17, 20, 54, or 56.*

5 kids ★★ Voodoo Doughnut. If one place embodies Portland's culture of eccentricity, it's this Old Town eatery where the art of deep-fried pastry circles is taken to new extremes. Doughnuts crusted with Captain Crunch and Fruit Loops sit next to Bacon Maple Bars (topped with real bacon) and the person-shaped Voodoo Doll, filled with raspberry jelly and impaled on a pretzel. If you can eat the giant Texas Challenge in under 80 seconds, it's free. Open 24 hours, Voodoo is popular with late-night revelers, and you can sometimes catch live music or a real live wedding going on, complete with coffee and doughnuts. A new location opened in 2011 at 1501 NE Davis St., complete with a bridge-crossing ceremony to transport the hallowed deep-frying oil. ⏱ *30 min. 22 SW 3rd Ave. ☎ 503/241-4704. www. voodoodoughnut.com. Open 24 hr. MAX: Skidmore Fountain. Bus: 12, 19, or 20.*

6 Mill Ends Park. Portland isn't just home to one of the largest urban parks (Forest Park) in the country; it also boasts the world's smallest, a patch of flowers 24 inches across in the median of SW Naito Parkway at Taylor Street. It started in 1948 when a newspaper journalist, whose office overlooked the road, planted flowers and began writing whimsical columns about a leprechaun named Patrick O'Toole who lived there with his family. It was formally recognized as a city park in 1976—on St. Patrick's Day, of course. *Open daily, free. MAX: Yamhill District. Bus: 15 or 51.*

The most atmospheric coffee-house in town, **7 Rimsky-Korsakoffee House** fills a former Victorian home with oddball art, moving tables, and decorated bathrooms you have to see to believe. The waiters are fun and sassy and the desserts, especially the sundaes, to die for. Some say the place is actually haunted. *707 SE 12th Ave. ☎ 503/232-2640. $.*

8 Stark's Vacuum Museum. Did you know they made vacuums out of cardboard during the Great Depression? You will after a visit to this display of powered cleaners through the ages, part of Stark's

The Voodoo Doll jelly doughnut.

Getting a fix at Rimsky-Korsakoffee House.

Vacuum Cleaner Sales & Service. Most of the 300 models were donated by locals, including hand-pumped ones from the 19th century (including one that took two people to operate) and retro-futuristic models from the space-age '60s. Careful—you might just be inspired to leave with a modern Hoover or Dyson. ⏱ *30 min. 107 NE Grand Ave.* ☎ *800/230-4101. www.starks. com. Free admission. Open Mon–Fri 8am–7pm; Sat 9am–5pm; Sun 11am–5pm. Bus: 6, 2, 19, or 20.*

⑨ Kidd's Toy Museum. Fans of antique playthings will love this private collection of hundreds, if not thousands, of toys, games, banks, and other trinkets dating as far back as the 1850s. Frank Kidd has filled one section of his auto parts warehouse with row upon row of vintage trains, soldiers, cars, and trucks. His mechanical cast-iron banks are worth a museum in themselves, with models that show a dentist extracting a tooth or kids peeking at a bathing beauty. (Parent alert: Some items are quite un-PC by modern standards.) Nothing is labeled, not even the building—look for a paper sign taped to the door—but Frank, who's often on-site, can give you details on just about anything in his singular collection, which includes dolls and teddy bears his wife has collected. ⏱ *1 hr. 1301 SE Grand Ave.* ☎ *503/233-7807. Free admission. Hours are officially Mon–Fri noon–6pm, but if you knock at other times you might find him in. Bus: 6.*

⑩ The Hat Museum. One of the country's largest collections of headgear fills a 1910 home in Ladd's Addition, once the home of a talented hatmaker. Over 1,300 hats for men and women, from antique Stetsons to modern tea hats, make up five distinct collections that span the globe. The tour (required) by owner Alyce Cornyn-Selby includes a wealth of detail on the history of hats and their creation, plus a $5 credit toward anything in the gift shop. Don't miss the novelty models, like the Thanksgiving table hat that sings and others that fold or hide things inside. The house itself is a curiosity, with secret spaces, mermaid ceiling paintings, and a couch made from a 1966 Cadillac. ⏱ *1½ hr. 1928 SE Ladd Ave.* ☎ *503/232-0433. www.thehat museum.com. Daily 10am–6pm. Tours required, $15 per person by prior appointment only. Bus: 10.*

⑪ ★ Mike's Museum of Motion Picture History. Film buffs know that Movie Madness is the best place in town to find videos and DVDs of classic, independent, and cult movies. It's also home to a collection of costumes and props from famous films, like the baby carriage from the stairway shootout in *The Untouchables* and an alien creature from *Mars Attacks*. Look for Julie Andrews' dress from *The Sound of Music* and Orson Welles' jacket from *Touch of Evil*, a classic 1958 film noir. 🕐 *45 min. 4320 SE Belmont St.* ☎ *503/234-4363. www. moviemadnessvideo.com/museum/ museum_main.htm. Sun–Thurs noon–11pm; Fri–Sat noon–midnight. Free admission. Bus: 15.*

Odd Events

At certain times of year, Portland's peculiarity spikes with annual events that celebrate the eccentric in each of us. On the first Saturday in March, the **Urban Iditarod** (www.keepportlandweird.org/ urbaniditarod) replaces huskies with people, sleds with shopping carts, and 1,000 miles through Alaska's frigid wastes with a 4-mile route across downtown Portland. (The date is the same, though.) Outlandish costumes are the rule and everyone's a winner. In mid-June, the 2-week annual bike festival known as Pedalpalooza includes Portland's contribution to the **World Naked Bike Ride,** consisting of thousands—that's right, *thousands*—of unclothed riders taking a lighthearted (and often chilly) spin around town. As seen below, the mid-August **Adult Soapbox Derby** (www.soapboxracer.com) updates the classic gravity cars of childhood with Ph.D.-level engineering, museum-quality art, and lots of beer. More than 5,000 people gather on the slopes of Mt. Tabor to watch cars hit speeds of over 50 mph, competing for prizes in decoration, velocity, and crowd-pleasing (pictured at right).

If you happen to see a large group of boisterous Santas careening around town in early December, chances are it's the latest incarnation of **SantaCon** (portland. cacophony.org), a mix of holiday spirit, performance art, and inebriated rowdiness organized by the Portland Cacophony Society (motto: "Life is short. Mess with someone else's").

Rainy Day Portland

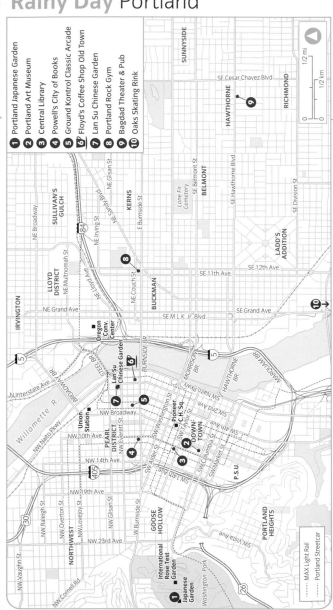

1. Portland Japanese Garden
2. Portland Art Museum
3. Central Library
4. Powell's City of Books
5. Ground Kontrol Classic Arcade
6. Floyd's Coffee Shop Old Town
7. Lan Su Chinese Garden
8. Portland Rock Gym
9. Bagdad Theater & Pub
10. Oaks Skating Rink

MAX Light Rail
Portland Streetcar

It's a fact of life: from fall through spring, and especially in the winter, Portland gets a lot of rain. (More than in famously wet Seattle, in fact.) But that doesn't mean there still isn't plenty to do when the clouds roll in and the misty Northwest drizzle starts. Most of the things on this tour are indoors, for obvious reasons, but a few outdoor ones take advantage of the moody change in atmosphere overcast skies can bring. So get out your rubber boots and rain jackets—Portlanders are notoriously averse to umbrellas—and head out. START: **MAX to Washington Park. Bus 63 on weekdays.**

❶ ★★ Portland Japanese Garden. Washington Park's flagship garden is just as enchanting— maybe more—in the rain as it is in the sun. Like most classical Japanese gardens, it's designed with the changing seasons in mind, with certain scenes best viewed in the rain (or snow, for that matter). The rough stones, meticulously trimmed shrubs, and placid koi pond take on a different, yet still serene, atmosphere of dripping leaves and rippling water. Just take care with some of the rock steps—they get very slippery. *See p 15,* ❶.

❷ ★ Portland Art Museum. Spend an hour indoors drying off with Marchel Duchamp, Gustave Courbet, Albert Bierstadt, and Ansel Adams—or at least their works—at this internationally recognized

institution. Time it right to catch a free gallery tour, lecture, or Midday Art Break. *Tours Sun–Fri 12:30pm and occasionally in the afternoon. See p 9,* ❷.

❸ ★ kids Central Library. The main branch of the Multnomah County Library, opened in 1913, fills a massive Georgian building downtown with 875 *tons* of books on over 17 miles of bookshelves. Just stepping inside is inspiring, with the sweeping main staircase climbing through a three-story atrium. The **Beverly Cleary Children's Library,** named after the famous local author, has a sculpture of Alice in Wonderland and a 14-foot bronze tree covered in carved images from kids' books like *The Wizard of Oz* and *The Little Engine That Could.* On the third floor, the **Collins Gallery**

Children's Room at Central Library.

hosts rotating art exhibits, and the **John Wilson Special Collections** focus on Pacific Northwest history, children's literature, and Native American books. ⏱ *1 hr. 801 SW 10th Ave.* ☎ *503/988-5123. www.multcolib.org. Mon, Thurs & Sat 10am–6pm; Tues & Wed 10am–8pm; Sun noon–5pm. Streetcar: Central Library. MAX: Library/SW 9th Ave.*

❹ ★★ kids **Powell's City of Books.** Put any lingering literary cravings to rest at Portland's world-class independent bookseller. Browse through 3,500 sections, including an outstanding **children's section** in the first-floor Rose Room. The **Basil Hallward Gallery,** upstairs in the Pearl Room, hosts new art exhibits every month, and the **World Cup coffee shop** has plenty of seats for browsing and watching the rain fall through the windowed walls. *See p 10,* ❸.

❺ ★ kids **Ground Kontrol Classic Arcade.** If (like me) you spent a good chunk of your childhood weekends in video arcades, this two-story retro game room will whisk you back to the days of honing your skills at Centipede and

Donkey Kong. Ground Kontrol has more than 90 cabinet games from the past 40 years, from oldies like Asteroids and Tempest to the newest, like the four-player Pac-Man Battle Royale. And they're all still only a quarter! Get a workout on Dance Dance Revolution in the back corner, or head upstairs for dozens of pinball machines. A full bar serves drinks and snacks, and DJs spin music in the evenings. On the third Thursday evening of every month, admission is $5 and all games are free. ⏱ *45 min. 511 NW Couch St.* ☎ *503/796-9364. www.groundkontrol.com. Free admission. Daily noon–2:30am, age 21 and over only after 5pm. MAX: NW 5th & Couch St.*

Serving Stumptown coffee in the ambiance of an old diner, ❻ **Floyd's Coffee Shop Old Town** (there's another one on the East Side) has comfy seating, inexpensive eats, and outstanding espresso drinks, perfect for a respite from the drizzle. *118 NW Couch St.* ☎ *503/295-7791. MAX: Old Town/Chinatown. Bus: 12, 19, or 20. $.*

Devotees at Powell's City of Books.

A meal at the classical Chinese Garden.

❼ ★★ Lan Su Chinese Garden. Like the Japanese Garden, this leafy escape in the heart of Chinatown was designed to be appreciated in any kind of weather. Covered walkways lead between pavilions with names like "Painted Boat in Misty Rain" and "Flowers Bathing in Spring Rain." Banana plants are positioned under rain gutters to create a distinctive sound when splashed with water. The Chinese Garden is a peaceful place to spend a damp afternoon, particularly the teahouse, where you can linger over a pot of Lapsang souchong and contemplate the central lake. *See p 16,* **❹**.

❽ Portland Rock Gym. Rock climbing in the rain? Sure, when it's inside the state's largest rock gym. Walls 35 feet high are studded with artificial climbing holds, offering an ever-changing selection of 100 climbing routes of all levels, each flagged with colored tape. In case you've never climbed before, they offer instruction and gear rental, as well as a weight room, cardio machines, and yoga and Pilates classes. Ropes are mandatory in the main room, but in the bouldering area you can learn this low-level skill (you're never more than a few feet off the padded floor) without being "tied in." Experts can tackle the 16-foot overhang or dozens of lead-climbing routes. 🕐 *1 hr. 21 NE 12th Ave.* ☎ *503/232-8310. www. portlandrockgym.com. Open Mon, Wed, Fri 11am–11pm; Tues & Thurs 7am–11pm; Sat 9am–9pm; Sun 9am–6pm. Day pass $15 adults ($10 before 3pm Mon–Fri), $7 children 11 and under or seniors 62 and older on weekdays ($10 weekends). Bus: 12, 19, 20, or 70.*

❾ ★ kids Bagdad Theater & Pub. Sometimes all you want to do on an overcast evening is eat pizza, drink beer, and watch a movie. This proud artifact of the Golden Age of Hollywood lets you do it in a little style. Built by Universal Pictures in 1927 for $100,000, it survived the transition from vaudeville to "talk-ies" and hosted everyone from Sammy Davis, Jr. to Jack Nicholson and Michael Douglas, here for the 1975 premiere of *One Flew Over the*

The Best Special-Interest Tours

Taking refuge at Bagdad Pub.

including wrought-iron fixtures, tiled arches, and paintings. The pub serves pizza, burgers, and hand-crafted ales, all of which you can bring into the theater for movies and the occasional comedy show or author reading. (Don't miss the Backstage Bar behind the screen, with its seven-story ceiling.) ⏱ *1–2 hr. 3702 SE Hawthorne Blvd.* ☎ *503/ 467-7521. www.mcmenamins.com/ bagdad. Admission $2–$28. Pub open Mon–Thurs 11am–midnight, Fri & Sat 11am–1am, Sun noon–mid-night. Backstage Bar open Mon–Thurs 5pm–midnight, Fri 5pm–2:30am, Sat 2pm–2:30am, Sun 2pm–midnight. Bus: 14.*

🔟 ★ **kids** **Oaks Skating Rink.** The weather is an afterthought inside the wooden skating rink at Oaks Amusement Park, open like the park itself since 1905. It's a roll through the halls of nostalgia, cir-cling the lovingly maintained floor beneath the working Wurlitzer pipe organ. You can rent skates, grab a snack, and even take a lesson on weekends. *See p 31,* 🔟. ●

Cuckoo's Nest. The McMenamin brothers restored the movie palace to all its faux-Middle Eastern glory,

Roller skating rink at Oaks Park Amusement Park.

Downtown Portland

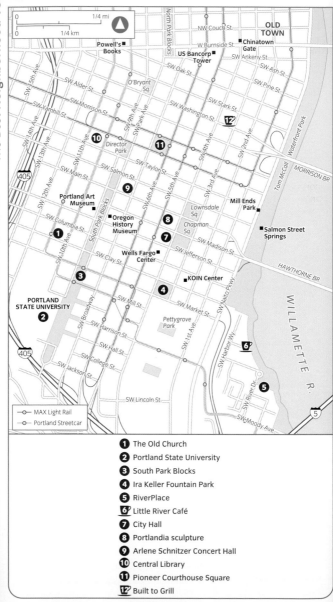

1. The Old Church
2. Portland State University
3. South Park Blocks
4. Ira Keller Fountain Park
5. RiverPlace
6. Little River Café
7. City Hall
8. Portlandia sculpture
9. Arlene Schnitzer Concert Hall
10. Central Library
11. Pioneer Courthouse Square
12. Built to Grill

Previous page: Deschutes Brewery in the Pearl District.

Downtown Portland is surprisingly compact and manageable for the heart of the state's largest city. Busy as it may be, it's still possible to bike from one end to the other in 10 minutes, traffic notwithstanding. Along with the concentration of offices and government buildings, it's home to Oregon's biggest university (Portland State) as well as plenty of shops, restaurants, and cultural venues to keep you entertained. Alternatives to walking are the MAX light rail, buses, or the streetcar. **START: Streetcar at SW 11th & Clay, bus: 6, 43, 45, 55, 58, or 68.**

❶ The Old Church. This Victorian beauty started as a Presbyterian church in 1883, making it one of the oldest buildings in the Pacific Northwest. Today it's owned by a nonprofit and hosts music concerts and other public events. Many of the original architectural features have been preserved, including the hand-carved fir pews and built-in umbrella racks (naturally) inside. ⏱ *30 min. 1422 SW 11th Ave.* ☎ *503/222-2031. www.oldchurch. org. Open Mon–Fri 11am–3pm. Self-guided tours are free; admission varies by scheduled event.*

❷ ★ Portland State University. With 30,000 students, the largest university in Oregon anchors the southern end of the South Park Blocks (see below) with its leafy 49-acre urban campus. A large percentage of the student body is older—the average age for undergrads is around 25—and many classes meet in the evenings and on weekends. Befitting its eco-conscious city home, PSU has a number of LEED-certified green buildings, including Lincoln Hall (SW Park Ave. and Mill St.) and the Engineering Building at SW 4th Avenue at College Street. ⏱ *30 min. Btw. SW Market St, SW 3rd Ave. & I-405.* ☎ *503/725-3000. www.pdx.edu.*

❸ ★★ South Park Blocks. Thank Portland cofounder Daniel Lownsdale for this strip of 12 grassy blocks leading from the PSU campus into the center of downtown. Four years after buying up most of what would become downtown Portland in 1848, Lownsdale donated the land to the city (some say, to guard his property from forest fires). The southernmost of the Park Blocks are

The nonprofit Old Church hosts a variety of events.

Chinese elephant statue, North Park Blocks.

home to the main Portland Farmer's Market on Saturdays from March to December (p 82). ⏱ *30 min. SW Park Ave. btw. Salmon & Hall sts. Open daily 5am–9pm.*

4 **kids** **Ira Keller Fountain Park.** This angular abstraction of a gushing mountain waterfall anchors a tree-packed park popular with PSU students. Some 13,000 gallons pour over every minute, and wading is encouraged; it's designed so you can walk to the top and look over (there's a 3-foot lip hidden under the water at the edge). ⏱ *30 min. SW 3rd Ave. & SW Clay St.*

5 ★ **RiverPlace.** Completed in 2001, the 50-acre development between the Marquam (I-5) and Hawthorne bridges combines condos,

townhomes, shops, and a hotel with a public marina basin and popular park on the west bank of the Willamette River. Here Portland's urban downtown meets its lifeblood river in a civilized way, with an extension of the riverfront pedestrian esplanade leading past a row of shops and restaurants, packed with people on sunny afternoons. The octagonal Newport Seafood Grill anchors the floating breakwater. ⏱ *1 hr. Btw. SW Harbor Way & SW Montgomery St. Streetcar: SW River Pkwy & Moody.*

Tasty soups and sandwiches are the order of the day at the snug **6** **Little River Café** in the middle of the RiverPlace esplanade. There's not much space inside, but

Benson Bubblers

In 1912, a local lumber baron and philanthropist named Simon Benson noticed his mill workers' breath smelled of booze. A teetotaler, Benson learned that fresh water was hard to find downtown, so he donated $10,000 to the city to install 20 bronze drinking fountains. (His ploy worked: beer consumption allegedly fell 25%.) There are now 52 "Benson bubblers" throughout Portland, mostly downtown, including the original four-bowl fountain at SW 5th Avenue and Washington Street. (Another 74 single-bowl variations were added later.) They're cleaned regularly and flow daily with fresh Bull Run drinking water.

the outside seats are great for watching local "dragonboats" paddle up and down the river. *315 SW Montgomery St. #310.* ☎ *503/227-2327. Hours vary with season; in summer 7am–8:30pm Mon–Thurs, 7am–9pm Fri—Sun. $.*

7 City Hall. Built in 1895, the home of Portland's City Council underwent a full renovation in the 1990s, restoring the four-story Italianate building to near its original glory. Commissioned artworks, both permanent and temporary, decorate the interior. ⏱ *30 min. 1221 SW 4th Ave.* ☎ *503/823-4000. www.portlandonline.com. 6am–7pm Mon–Fri.*

8 Portlandia sculpture. Before there was *Portlandia* the show, there was Portlandia the sculpture: the second-largest hammered-copper statue of its kind in the world, after the Statue of Liberty. Based on the city seal, the 34-foot-high "Lady Commerce" kneels over the entrance to the Portland Building, holding a trident in one hand and reaching down with the other. *1120 SW 5th Ave. btw. Madison & Main sts.*

9 ★★ Arlene Schnitzer Concert Hall. The most spectacular of the three properties that make up the Portland Center for the Performing Arts, "the Schnitz," as it's known locally, is the last of the grand old theaters that once lined Broadway. It was built in 1928 and fully restored in 1984 to all of its original Italian Rococo Revival splendor inside and out, starting with the distinctive 65-foot "Portland" sign lit with more than 5,000 lights. There's seating for 2,776, an orchestra pit, and a statue of a scantily clad woman with her hands over her face called "Surprise." (She lost two fingers during a gunfight that broke out during a movie in the 1950s.) Performances held here include the Oregon Symphony, the White Bird Dance Company, and various art programs and lectures. *1037 SW Broadway at Main St.* ☎ *503/248-4335. www.pcpa.com. Ticket prices and showtimes vary.*

🔟 ★ kids Central Library. There's something for everyone at the Multnomah County Library's main branch. The Georgian building itself is worth a look, with its central staircase, three-story atrium, and cozy children's library. *See p 39,* ❸.

⓫ ★ kids Pioneer Courthouse Square. Shoemaker Elijah Hill purchased this downtown block in 1849 for $24 and a pair of high boots. Since then it's hosted the city's first school, the second oldest federal courthouse in the West, and, today, more visitors than any other place in Portland. For people-watching, it can't be beat. *See p 9,* ❶.

The competition is stiff, but the ⓬ **Built to Grill** food cart gets repeat votes as one of Portland's best, serving hot Italian sandwiches and pasta dishes like bowtie primavera in one of the city's first cart "pods." *SW 3rd Ave. & SW Washington St.* ☎ *503/789-3767. $.*

Checkmate at Pioneer Square.

The Pearl District

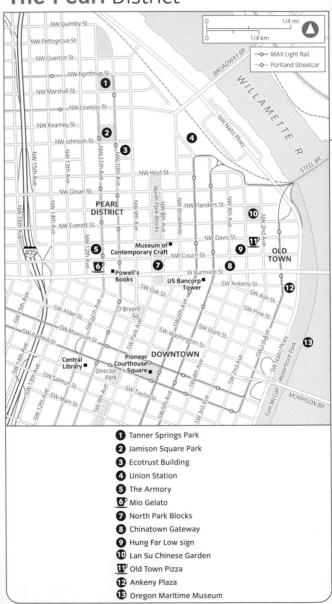

0   1/4 mi
0   1/4 km

—○— MAX Light Rail
—○— Portland Streetcar

1 Tanner Springs Park
2 Jamison Square Park
3 Ecotrust Building
4 Union Station
5 The Armory
6 Mio Gelato
7 North Park Blocks
8 Chinatown Gateway
9 Hung Far Low sign
10 Lan Su Chinese Garden
11 Old Town Pizza
12 Ankeny Plaza
13 Oregon Maritime Museum

Portland's innermost neighborhoods in the northeast quadrant run the gamut from the upscale art galleries, eateries, and condos of the swank Pearl district to the slightly more disheveled streets of Old Town and Chinatown. Together, they make a great walking route that takes you from the energetic campus of Portland State University to the meditative pathways of the Lan Su Chinese Garden in Chinatown. Once a grubby district of warehouses and light industry, "the Pearl" is a case study in urban revitalization, while Old Town holds on to its history, at least architecturally. (By the way, "Couch" street is pronounced "cooch," not like the piece of furniture.) START: **Streetcar NW 10th and Marshall; Bus 77.**

❶ Tanner Springs Park. A quiet haven of burbling water and reedy grasses, this park re-creates a pocket of Portland's original wetlands. A walking trail leads past benches along a creek, and the east edge is lined with a wall-like art installation of old rail tracks interspersed with blue glass made by a local company. 🕐 *15 min. NW Marshall & 11th aves.*

❷ kids ★ Jamison Square Park. Just 2 blocks away is another water-centric park, this one focused on a large fountain designed to mimic a tidal pool. Water spills over a series of low steps into a shallow pool that periodically empties and refills. Look for the statue of a brown bear made from smooth red granite; he's named *Rico Pasado*, meaning "rich past." 🕐 *15 min. NW Johnson & 10th aves.*

❸ ★ Ecotrust Building. One of the greenest of Portland's green buildings is home to a collection of suitable sustainable businesses and nonprofits, including a Patagonia store and offices of the conservation group that gives the building its unofficial name. (Officially, it's the Jean Vollum Natural Capital Center.) During the 2001 renovation of this 1895 warehouse, some 98% of the construction waste was recycled or reclaimed. Look for portions of the original building's facade that still

stand along NW 10th Avenue. *See* *p 11,* ❹.

❹ ★ Union Station. Portland's grand rail terminal, built in 1896, reflected the city's position at the western end of the only sea-level route through the Cascades. The Italian Renaissance–style building was renovated in 1996 after a century of use, and now serves train and intercity bus travelers. Luckily, it kept its signature 150-foot Romanesque clock tower, just with the addition of a neon "Go By Train" sign; you can get a taste of the

Union Station clock tower.

Tanner Springs Park.

building's glory days inside at Amtrak's only first-class Metropolitan Lounge on the West Coast, as well as at **Wilfs,** 800 NW 6th Ave. (☎ **503/223-0070,** www.wilfs restaurant.com), which combines turn-of-the-century ambience with organic local produce and live jazz from Wednesday through Saturday

Entrance to Chinatown.

night. 🕐 *30 min. 800 NW 6th Ave. at Irving St.* ☎ *503/273-4865.*

5 ★ **The Armory.** Yet another example of a historic building saved from the wrecking ball and repurposed, this unmistakable brick fortress anchors the downtown "Brewery Blocks." Constructed in 1891 to house the Oregon National Guard, it hosted presidential speeches, symphony concerts, and many, many casks of beer over the next century. A 2006 renovation made it one of the greenest buildings in the country—we're talking LEED platinum status—and the new home of Portland Center Stage, the city's largest theater company. The striking building now holds the 600-seat **Gerding Theater,** a small **studio theater,** and a **cafe.** Step into the huge lobby to see the grand staircase cantilevered off the second-floor balcony and the enormous ceiling trusses that give it such a roomy feel. 🕐 *15 min. 128 NW 11th Ave. at Davis St.* ☎ *503/445-3700. www.pcs.org. Ticket prices and showtimes vary.*

Chinatown's iconic arch and Hung Far Low sign.

Recharge at **6 Mio Gelato** with a double scoop of Italian gelato (mascarpone and tiramisu? mango and strawberry?) and a shot of espresso—or, if you're feeling hungry, a bowl of soup or panini sandwich. 🕐 *15 min. 25 NW 11th Ave.* ☎ *503/226-8002. $.*

7 kids ★ North Park Blocks. Disconnected from their southern counterparts despite a 19th-century lawsuit, the North Park Blocks have a more urban feel, even though they have just as many old trees lining their sidewalks. The playground and basketball court are both popular, as are the various artworks: the 12-foot bronze elephant sculpture between Burnside and Couch streets is an oversize replica of a Shang Dynasty wine pitcher, a gift to the city from a Chinese foundry owner. Photographer William Wegman, of Weimaraner dog fame, designed the checkerboard granite tiles of the "Portland Dog Bowl"

between Davis and Everett streets to mimic a linoleum kitchen floor. Think of the bronze water bowl as a canine counterpart to the Benson bubbler fountains (p 46). 🕐 *30 min. NW Park Ave. from Ankeny St. to Glisan St. Open daily 5am–9pm.*

8 Chinatown Gateway. This ornate arch was built in 1985, an impressive monument to the long history of Portland's Chinese residents. Artisans from Taiwan put it together and installed the two lions on either side. (The one on the left, Yin, protects the young, and Yang, the one on the right, protects the country.) The 38-foot high structure is decorated with 78 dragons and 58 mythical characters, including the Chinese characters for "Portland Chinatown" on the south side and "Four Seas, One Family" on the north side. 🕐 *5 min. NW 4th Ave. at Burnside St.*

9 Hung Far Low sign. Chinatown's other landmark earns its share of giggles, but this pagoda-topped

White Stag Sign

One of Portland's most distinctive symbols greets drivers and cyclists crossing the Burnside Bridge into downtown: a bounding neon stag above the words "Portland Oregon," enclosed by an outline of the state. The wording has gone through more revisions than a breakup letter, starting in 1940 when it was built to advertise White Satin Sugar. The building's next tenant conveniently shared an adjective, so the sign read "White Stag Sportswear" until 1995, when it was changed to read "Made in Oregon," with "Old Town" the latest subtitle. The current arrangement went up in 2010. (If you're around during the holidays, notice how easily the stag is transformed into Rudolph the Red-Nosed Reindeer.)

marquee did advertise a real restaurant that stood here from 1928 to 2005. (Like many Chinese-owned businesses in Portland, it relocated to SE 82nd Ave.) The two-story, 2,000-pound neon sign, a beloved local icon, was restored and–ahem–re-erected in 2010. ⏲ 5 min. NW 4th Ave. at Couch St.

🔟 ★★ Lan Su Chinese Garden. Complete your Chinatown trifecta with a stop at this astonishingly authentic garden, occupying a full block on the neighborhood's eastern side. You'll feel like you've stepped off a boat in ancient Suzhou, the coastal Chinese city where the entire shebang was designed, packed up, and exported to be reassembled here in 2001. In the lakeside Tower of Cosmic Reflections, the pagoda-style Teahouse (☎ 503/224-8455) offers a contemplative spot to watch the light change over the plantings and classical Chinese buildings. See p 16, ❹.

The Pearl District Saturday Market.

At the distinctive **11 Old Town Pizza,** a pizzeria housed in a former hotel, step up to the old reception desk to order a slice, and keep an eye out for Nina, the resident ghost. *15 min. 226 NW Davis St. ☎ 503/222-9999. $.*

12 Ankeny Plaza. Once the city's nexus of business and entertainment, this triangular plaza in Old Town is now home to the **Portland Saturday Market** of craft vendors and the 14-foot bronze and granite **Skidmore Fountain,** the oldest piece of public art in the city. For the fountain's grand opening in 1888, local brewer Henry Weinhard offered to pump beer through it using firehoses, but for some reason city leaders turned him down. Many of the nearby buildings, built of brick and cast iron in the late 19th century, are part of the Skidmore/

Old Town National Historic District. *SW 1st Ave. & SW Ankeny St.*

13 ★ kids Oregon Maritime Museum. The steam-powered sternwheeler tug, *Portland,* the last of its kind to operate in the U.S., was retired in 1981 after 3 decades of service and restored to house a collection of maritime artifacts, ship models, and other nautical memorabilia. There's a children's corner with a working ship's whistle and other hands-on goodies. The ship itself is the real attraction, though, as you'll discover on a tour as one of the expert docents takes you from pilot house to engine room. *45 min. On the Willamette River in Waterfront Park, at Pine St. ☎ 503/224-7724. www.oregon maritimemuseum.org. Open Wed–Sat 11am–4pm; Sun 12:30–4:30pm. Admission $5 adults, $4 seniors 62 and over & children 6–17.*

Northwest Portland

NORTHWEST INDUSTRIAL

NW Nicolai St

NW Reed St

NW Front Ave

NW York St

MAX Light Rail
Portland Streetcar

NW Wilson St

7

NW Vaughn St

30

NW Thurman St

6

NW 25th Ave

NW Sevier St

NW Raleigh St

NW 19th Ave

NW 18th Ave

NW 14th Ave

*Wallace
Park*

NW Quimby St

NW 22nd Ave

NW Pettygrove St

NW Overton St

NW 20th Ave

NW Northrup St

NW Marshall St

NORTHWEST

NW Lovejoy St

NW 24th Ave

NW 17th Ave

1

4

NW Kearney St

2

NW Johnson St

NW 23rd Ave

NW 21st Ave

NW Irving St

3

NW Westover Rd

NW Hoyt St
Couch Park

NW 15th Ave

5

NW Glisan St

NW Flanders St

NW Trinity Pl

NW 16th Ave

NW Everett St

NW Davis St

405

NW Couch St

*WASHINGTON
PARK*

W Burnside St

SW Alder St

SW Vista Ave

SW St. Clair Ave

SW King Ave

SW 21st Ave

SW 20th Ave

SW 18th Ave

SW Morrison St

■
**Jeld-Wen
Field**

SW Park Pl

GOOSE HOLLOW

1. Northwest 23rd Avenue
2. Northwest 21st Avenue
3. Northwest 20th Avenue historic houses
4. 3D Center of Art and Photography
5. Mission Theater & Pub
6. Steven Smith Teamaker
7. Clear Creek Distillery

Portland's northwest corner is a neighborhood of tree-shaded Victorian homes, postwar apartment buildings, and modern mansions overlooking downtown and the river. It's one of the city's wealthier districts, more compact than the east side without feeling claustrophobic—on the contrary, with Arlington Heights and Forest Park rising to the west, it feels more like you're on the edge of a forest. Young professionals have started moving in—those that can afford to, anyway—and visitors come by the truckload for the varied shopping and dining options on NW 21st and 23rd avenues. It's easy to navigate, especially in the "Alphabet District" where the street names are ordered accordingly. START: **Bus: 15 or 77; Streetcar: NW 23rd & Marshall.**

1 ★★ **Northwest 23rd Ave.** From West Burnside to Thurman Street, NW 23rd Avenue is an almost continuous string of restaurants, cafes, boutiques, coffee shops, bars, and markets. Detractors may dismiss it as "trendy-third," but it's the commercial heart of this part of town, and definitely one of the best shopping and dining stretches in Portland. The south end near Burnside is home to larger chain stores like Pottery Barn and Urban Outfitters. As you head north, you'll find more distinctive local places like **Gilt Jewelry** (720 NW 23rd Ave. at Johnson St.), **Two Tarts Bakery** (2309 NW Kearney St. at 23rd Ave.), and **Shogun's Gallery** (1111 NW 23rd Ave. at

Marshall St.). Things peter out around Thurman Street, but take a left (west) for another 6 long blocks of options, plus, eventually, one of the main entrances to Forest Park. 🕐 *1½ hr.*

2 ★ **Northwest 21st Ave.** Two blocks east, NW 21st Avenue is similar to 23rd but leans more toward the food side of things. Take your pick from outstanding American fare at **Lucy's Table** (704 NW 21st Ave. at Irving St.), Italian at **Caffe Mingo** (807 NW 21st Ave. at Kearney St.), with its chic bar next door, or French cooking at **Paley's Place** (1204 NW 21st Ave. at Northrup St.). The **Chop Butchery & Charcuterie**

23rd Avenue shopping.

23rd Avenue display.

(735 NW 21st Ave. at Johnson St.) offers all things meat. It's not all about eating, though; **Cinema 21** (616 NW 21st Ave. at Irving St.) shows independent and art-house movies. 🕐 *1½ hr.*

❸ **Northwest 20th Avenue historic houses.** Gorgeous homes are everywhere up here, but you can find three excellent examples within a few blocks of Irving Street on 20th Avenue. (Keep in mind they're all private homes.) The 1892 Richardsonian Romanesque Revival at 615 NW 20th Ave. at Hoyt Street has the slate shingles, substantial stonework, and arched entrance porch that recall other examples of the style such as Trinity Church in Boston and the American Museum of Natural History in New York City. The 1908 Colonial Revival at 733 NW 20th Ave. at Johnson Street was designed after a mid-18th-century Georgian colonial home in Pennsylvania, and the 1910 Craftsman at 811 NW 20th Ave. at Johnson Street is another example of the simple but handsome style. 🕐 *30 min.*

❹ **kids** **3D Center of Art and Photography.** A small but comprehensive museum and gallery of 3-D images shows the long trail of trial and error it took to bring about

The Simpsons in Portland?

If some of the street names in this part of town sound familiar, thank local son Matt Groening, creator of the TV hits *The Simpsons* and *Futurama,* who grew up in the Rose City. In the Alphabet District, look for (Montgomery) Burnside, (Ned) Flanders, (Reverend) Lovejoy, and (Mayor) Quimby Streets. The Springfield Gorge and the Murderhorn, Springfield's highest peak, echo the Columbia River Gorge and Mt. Hood. And the benighted nuclear power plant where Homer Simpson works may have been based on the Trojan Nuclear Power Plant in Rainier, 46 miles north. It was decommissioned after 16 years due to safety and seismic concerns. D'oh!

the eye-popping movie spectacles of today. Learn about 3-D's 160-year history, from the Civil War to the Space Program, and once you understand how the process works, watch an experimental film or two in the theater. *See p 28,* **4**.

The singular **5** **Mission Theater & Pub** started as a Swedish Evangelical Mission in 1912, then served as a Longshoreman's Union hall before becoming Oregon's first theater-pub. Sit in the balcony or on the floor for recent movies, cult films, live music, or sporting events projected on a big screen. It's a McMenamins joint, so, of course, pub fare, handcrafted ales, and wine are on sale. Wednesday is "Burger, Beer & a Movie" night, a cheap date at just $12 per person. *1 hr. 1624 NW Glisan St. at 17th Ave.* ☎ *503/223-4527. www. mcmenamins.com. Admission $3 adults, $1 children 11 and under, Age 21 and over only for shows after 9pm. Event hours vary.*

6 **Steven Smith Teamaker.** The local founder of both Stash Tea

and Tazo Tea has launched his own line of small-batch teas using rare, high-quality ingredients. You can come by the facility, an old blacksmith shop, to taste a cup or see the teas being made and packaged. If you're inspired, you can even blend your own batch. *30 min. 1626 NW Thurman St.* ☎ *503/719-8752 or 800/624-9531. www.smith tea.com. Open Mon–Fri 9am–5pm. Free admission.*

7 **Clear Creek Distillery.** Traditional European brandy-making techniques meet northwest Oregon's bounty of fruit at this artisan distillery, producer of fruit eaux de vie, grappas, and wine brandies. They only offer public tours around Memorial Day and Thanksgiving, but their tasting room and store are open year-round. Come by to learn about the process and sample spirits like their pear eaux de vie, with the pear grown inside the bottle, or their Islay-style Oregon single malt whiskey. *30 min. 2389 NW Wilson St.* ☎ *503/248-9470. www.clearcreek distillery.com. Open Mon–Sat 9am–5pm. Free admission.*

Quality check of pear eaux de vie, Clear Creek Distillery.

Northeast Alberta Street

1/4 mi
1/4 km

- 1 Community Cycling Center
- 2 One Stop Sustainability Shop
- 3' Random Order Coffeehouse & Bakery
- 4 Vernon Tank Playground
- 5 Movie Marvel Museum
- 6 Guardino Gallery
- 7 Alberta Rose Theatre
- 8 McMenamins Kennedy School

N ortheast Alberta Street between 12th and 33r
otherwise known as the Alberta Arts District, is or
neighborhoods outside the city center. Recently it has
spot for young professionals looking for affordable rea
cultural mix that can be lacking in the rest of the city. Hisp
and African-American businesses rub shoulders with hip cafes, chic
boutiques, and outstanding eateries. And on the last Thursday of
every month, the street is closed to traffic for a combination art walk
and street party. **START: Bus 8 or 72.**

❶ Community Cycling Center.
Few places embody Portland's two-
wheeled ethos in such an admirable
way as this nonprofit bike shop.
They don't just fix and sell bikes,
parts, and accessories—they also
offer year-round programs that help
get citizens up and rolling, including
bike camps, bike clubs, mainte-
nance classes, and bike drives for
low-income families. ⏲ *15 min.
1700 NE Alberta St. at 17th Ave.
☎ 503/287-8786. www.community
cyclingcenter.org. Open Tues–Sun
10am–6pm.*

❷ One Stop Sustainability Shop.
One of Portland's most common
buzzwords may mystify some, but
not after a visit to this store, which
offers everything from cleaning products to toys and pet beds. It's run
by a friendly mother-and-daughter

team who are happy to explain the
reasoning and philosophy behind
selling things that are nontoxic, fair-
trade, recycled, and/or biodegrad-
able, and often locally made. They
also frequently offer classes. ⏲ *30
min. 1468 NE Alberta St. ☎ 503/241-
5404. Open Tues–Fri 10am–6pm; Sat
& Sun 10am–5pm.*

Refuel at **❸ Random Order
Coffeehouse & Bakery** with a cup
of java and a slice of homemade pie,
either sweet or savory. Brandied
peach and salted caramel apple are
both specialties, and the Catalan
vegetable potpie is enough for a
meal. *1800 NE Alberta St. at 18th
Ave. ☎ 971/340-6995. Open Mon
6:30am–8pm; Tues–Sun 6:30am–
11pm. $.*

Last Thursday celebration on Alberta Street.

Portland Fruit Tree Project

This local nonprofit tackles the persistent problem of access to healthy food with one of those ideas that seems so obvious in hindsight: Organize volunteers to harvest fruit and nuts from trees around the city, produce that would otherwise go to waste, and distribute it to people in need through local food pantries. In 2010, they harvested almost 30,000 pounds of fruit, mostly on private residential properties, and supplied it to over 2,900 families in need. They also keep a constantly updated fruit tree registry and hold workshops to teach people to care for them. ☎ *503/284-6106; www.portlandfruit.org*.

④ kids Vernon Tank Playground. This small park and playground sit in the shadow of two huge cylindrical water tanks that look like something out of *War of the Worlds*. It's an odd mix, but it works; if the kids get tired of the swings and slides, you can play escape-the-invaders-from-outer-space instead. 🕓 *30 min. NE 21st Ave. & Prescott St. Open 5am–10pm.*

⑤ kids Movie Marvel Museum. More "gallery" than "museum," this tiny place is chock-full of memorabilia covering the entire history of cinema, from historical photos and hand-cranked silent movie projectors to a five-seat old-timey mini-theater with shorts and cartoons playing continuously. You can't miss the full-size C-3PO and Frankenstein's lab. 🕓 *45 min. 2728 NE Alberta St. at 28th Ave.* ☎ *503/280-2376. www.movie marvelmuseum.com. Admission $3.50 adults, $2.50 children 12 and under. Open Sat 1–9 pm.*

The classy McMenamins Kennedy School hotel.

Guest room at the Kennedy School.

6 Guardino Gallery. Of all the galleries on Alberta Street, Guardino has the most reliably exciting mix of works and styles. From bronze sculptures and acrylic paintings to prints made with rusted car parts on old silk, there's always something unexpectedly intriguing on display. In the same building, you'll find the **HiiH Gallery,** selling handmade paper lamps; **Redbird Studio,** with handmade cards, stationery, clothes, and crafts; and **Suzette,** a creperie. ⏱ *1 hr. 2939 NE Alberta St. at 29th Ave.* ☎ *503/281-9048. www.guardinogallery.com. Open Tues 11am–5pm; Wed–Sat 11am–6pm; Sun 11am–4pm.*

7 ★ Alberta Rose Theatre. Yet another lovingly resurrected old theater, the 300-seat Alberta Rose started as a motion picture house in 1927, operated until 1978, and was reborn as a space for independent films, comedy, acoustic music, and other live performances. They serve regional libations and handmade Australian-style pies and other snacks. If you can, catch one of the regular tapings of *Live Wire! Radio,* a modern take on multi-performer vaudeville shows. ⏱ *2 hr. 3000 NE Alberta St. at 30th Ave.* ☎ *503/719-6055. www.albertarosetheatre.com. Showtimes vary, and some performances are age 21 and over only.*

8 ★★ McMenamins Kennedy School. Detention never sounded as appealing as it does at this 1912 grade school, renovated and reopened in 1997 as a combination hotel, restaurant, and movie theater. There are no less than five bars on the premises, including the Detention Bar, Honors Bar, and the Boiler Room, all serving beer from the on-site brewery and other alcoholic tipples. Thirty-five guest rooms fill former classrooms, and the walls are covered in original art and historical photos. Relax in the hot outdoor soaking pool or catch a matinee on a couch in the second-run movie theater. *5736 NE 33rd Ave.* ☎ *503/249-3983. www.mc menamins.com.*

Hawthorne & Belmont

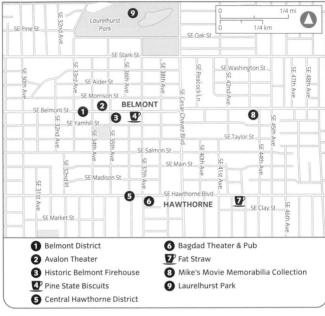

1. Belmont District
2. Avalon Theater
3. Historic Belmont Firehouse
4. Pine State Biscuits
5. Central Hawthorne District
6. Bagdad Theater & Pub
7. Fat Straw
8. Mike's Movie Memorabilia Collection
9. Laurelhurst Park

The giant sunflower painted at the intersection of SE 33rd Avenue and Yamhill Street captures the friendly, community-minded spirit of this part of town, where downtown can seem a world away, even though it's just a 5-minute drive across the river. The vibe here is more suburban, with tree-lined streets and sometimes as much bicycle traffic as cars and trucks. These neighborhoods are popular among young renters and families with kids, and everyone congregates on the busy sidewalks of Hawthorne Boulevard and Belmont Street. Side streets are perfect for rambling or rolling (Salmon St. has a busy bike lane). START: **Bus 14 or 15.**

---

1 ★ Belmont District. The commercial district on Southeast Belmont Street is tiny compared to Hawthorne, but it packs a lot into just a few blocks. You'll find shopping at eclectic places like **Noun** (3300 SE Belmont St. at 33rd Ave.), a quirky housewares/antiques store, and **Palace** (828 SE 34th Ave. at Belmont St.), with upscale new and

vintage clothing for men and women. Hungry? Grab a great burger at **Dick's Kitchen** (3312 SE Belmont St. at 33rd Ave.) and dessert at **Saint Cupcake,** which shares a storefront with Noun. Thirsty? **The Tao of Tea** (3430 SE Belmont St. at 34th Ave.) is Portland's oldest teahouse, and **Stumptown Coffee Roasters** (3356 SE

Belmont St. at 33rd Ave.) offers great people-watching and free coffee cuppings (aka tastings) daily at noon and 2pm in their Annex two doors down. For nightlife, try the Avalon Theater (see below) or head downstairs to the **Blue Monk** (3341 SE Belmont St. at 33rd Ave.) for jazz and blues. *1 hr. SE Belmont St. from 33rd to 35th aves.*

② kids **Avalon Theater.** Second-run movies and nickel arcade games—is there any better way to stretch your date dollars? Oregon's oldest theater was also the first in the state with more than one screen. Now it shows films on three screens and fills the rest of the space with skee-ball, air hockey, and video games. You can even redeem your skee-ball tickets for prizes and candy. *1 hr. 3451 SE Belmont St. at 34th Ave. ☎ 503/238-1617. Sun–Fri noon–midnight; 11am–midnight Sat Movies are $2.75 for adults, $2.25 for seniors and children 11 and under. Games are 20¢, but you have to pay admission to play.*

❸ kids **Historic Belmont Firehouse.** Kids and history buffs love this 1912 firehouse, now home to a safety learning center and museum to Portland's firefighting history. Restored antique gear and equipment, like an 1859 Jeffers Sidestroke Handpump Fire Engine, are on display and, often, touchable. There's even a fire pole to slide down! *45 min. 900 SE 35th Ave. at 34th Ave. ☎ 503/823-3615. www.jeffmorris foundation.org. Open the 2nd Sat of every month, except July, Aug, and Dec, 10am–3pm or by previous appointment.*

There's almost always a line out the door at cozy little **④** **Pine State Biscuits,** which is evidence both of how tasty their homemade buttermilk biscuits are and how few tables await inside. Their "reggie deluxe"— fried chicken, bacon, cheese, an egg, and gravy on a biscuit—was voted one of the country's best sandwiches by no less than *Esquire* magazine. *3640 SE Belmont St. at 35th Ave. ☎ 503/236-3346. $.*

Stumptown Roasters.

Presents of Mind.

5 ★ **Central Hawthorne District.** It's hard to beat Hawthorne Boulevard from 34th to 39th avenues for strollable shopping, eating, and entertainment. The whole commercial stretch runs roughly from 30th to 50th avenues, with everything from brewpubs to vintage clothing stores. The heart of it is in the high 30s, especially the block between 36th and 37th avenues, where you'll find the historic Bagdad Theater & Pub (see below), a branch of **Powell's Books** (3723 SE Hawthorne Blvd. at 36th Ave.) specializing in home and garden titles, and **Pastaworks** (3735 SE Hawthorne Blvd. at 36th Ave.), a European-style grocery and deli with an on-site eatery called **Evoe.** (You'll also find a good number of dreadlocked buskers, but they're usually innocuous.) Other spots worth a stop are **Presents of Mind** (3633 SE Hawthorne Blvd. at 36th Ave.) for all things gift-oriented, **Imelda's and Louie's** (3426 SE Hawthorne Blvd. at 34th Ave.) for women's and men's shoes, and the **Dollar Scholar** (3343 SE Hawthorne Blvd. at 33rd Ave.) for bargain-basement fun. ⏲ *2 hr. SE Hawthorne Blvd. btw. 34th & 39th aves.*

Pick your poison in Bagdad.

6 ★ **kids** **Bagdad Theater & Pub.** One of Portland's grandest old theaters, veteran of some 25,000 shows over the decades, is now the main anchor of the Hawthorne commercial district. You can see a movie or show inside, knock back a tipple at one of two bars (including one behind the screen), or enjoy a meal and craft-brewed beer at the restaurant, which spills out onto the sidewalk in good weather. The building itself is eye-popping inside, restored to the full opulence of its inauguration in 1927, minus the spouting fountain. *See p 41,* **9**.

The name **7** **Fat Straw** will make sense when you order your first glass of "boba" (bubble tea), an addictive milky Asian concoction with tapioca balls on the bottom. The less adventurous can go with fresh avocado or coconut-mango smoothies, or regular tea or coffee, and for noshing they serve tasty *bahn mi* (Vietnamese sandwiches). *4258 SE Hawthorne Blvd. at 42nd Ave.* ☎ *503/233-3369. $.*

8 ★ **Mike's Movie Memorabilia Collection.** Ever wonder what happened to the knife from the shower scene in Hitchcock's *Psycho* or the monster costume from *Young Frankenstein?* They're here, inside the Movie Madness video store, along with other one-of-a-kind cinematic costumes and props. *See p 37,* **11**.

9 ★ **kids** **Laurelhurst Park.** Sometimes all you need at the end of a good walk is a shady patch of grass, maybe with a playground for the kids or a duck pond nearby. Look no further—Laurelhurst Park has all these and more, including a picnic grove, a hillside of rhododendrons, and trees that wouldn't be out of place on the slopes of Mt. Hood. Designed by a disciple of the Olmsted Brothers' natural approach, Laurelhurst became the first city park to be listed on the National Register of Historic Places in 2001. There's an off-leash area for dogs and, across Stark Street, a children's playground next to tennis and basketball courts. (Originally, girls were supposed to play on the north side and boys on the south.) *See p 24,* **7**.

View of downtown and Hawthorne Bridge from the esplanade.

Inner Southeast

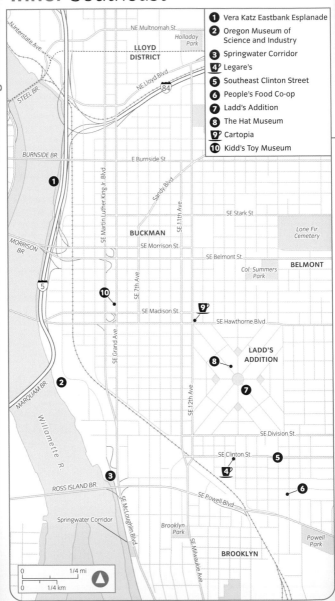

1 Vera Katz Eastbank Esplanade
2 Oregon Museum of Science and Industry
3 Springwater Corridor
4 Legare's
5 Southeast Clinton Street
6 People's Food Co-op
7 Ladd's Addition
8 The Hat Museum
9 Cartopia
10 Kidd's Toy Museum

NE Multnomah St.

Holladay Park

LLOYD DISTRICT

NE Lloyd Blvd.

N Interstate Ave.

STEEL BR.

BURNSIDE BR.

E Burnside St.

Sandy Blvd.

SE Stark St.

SE Martin Luther King Jr. Blvd.

SE 11th Ave.

BUCKMAN

MORRISON BR.

SE Morrison St.

Lone Fir Cemetery

SE Belmont St.

BELMONT

SE 7th Ave.

Col. Summers Park

SE Madison St.

SE Hawthorne Blvd.

LADD'S ADDITION

MARQUAM BR.

Willamette R.

SE Grand Ave.

SE 12th Ave.

SE Division St.

SE Clinton St.

ROSS ISLAND BR.

SE Powell Blvd.

SE McLoughlin Blvd.

Springwater Corridor

Brooklyn Park

SE Milwaukie Ave.

Powell Park

BROOKLYN

0   1/4 mi
0   1/4 km

Portland's innermost Southeast district starts with industrial warehouses near the river, but these soon give way to the mostly residential Hosford-Abernethy neighborhood, with a distinctly liberal, eco-conscious bent. Cooperative gardens, alternative schools, and chicken coops are the norm around here, and you'll see more bicycles and baby strollers on the streets than cars. Small commercial hubs along Clinton and Division streets combine restaurants, coffee shops, and unique local businesses like Langlitz Leathers, creators of the first custom leather motorcycle jacket in 1947, and Loprinzi's Gym, an ultra-old-school bodybuilding facility nearby.

START: **Bus 4, 6, 10, 14, 15, 31, 32, or 33.**

1 ★★ **kids** **Vera Katz Eastbank Esplanade.** Start on the east bank of the Willamette, where this paved path runs for 1.5 miles from the Hawthorne Bridge to the Steel Bridge, with great river-level views of the city's downtown skyline. Along the trail you'll pass public art, map markers, and interpretive panels on the history of the river and the area. A 1,200-foot floating walkway, the longest of its kind in the country, leads under the Burnside Bridge and past a public boat dock. (If you have time, the entire 2-mile loop across the Steel and Hawthorne bridges and through Tom McCall Waterfront Park is a Portland must-do.) **Note:** The esplanade is named for German-born Vera Katz, who was the first woman to serve as the Speaker of the Oregon House of Representatives and was the 45th Mayor of Portland. 🕑 *30 min.*

2 ★ **kids** **Oregon Museum of Science and Industry.** At the southern end of the esplanade, "OMSI" boasts all the science-themed learning options you could ask for, from the hands-on exhibits,

Biking down the Eastbank Esplanade.

Artifacts at OMSI.

planetarium, and IMAX theater inside to an actual submarine moored in the river. This end of the Eastbank Esplanade, under the Marquam Bridge that carries I-5, is particularly pretty on sunny days, with views of the Hawthorne Bridge and the South Waterfront. 🕐 *1 hr. See p 18,* **7**.

③ Springwater Corridor. From OMSI, it's just a few blocks to the start of this 21-mile multiuse recreation trail that leads south and east through Sellwood to the town of Boring (seriously). It's part of a 40-mile paved loop that circles the entire city, but it's worth exploring even just the beginning of the trail, which follows the old trolley train tracks along the surprisingly green and quiet riverbank. **Note:** The restored Linneman Trolley Station near Southeast Powell and 185th is a convenient trailhead at which to park your car, fill your water bottles, or to use the public restrooms. Another Springwater pitstop is at Southeast 136th, where a small market serves up liquid refreshment to thirsty trail warriors. 🕐 *30 min.*

Minuscule **④ Legare's** on Clinton Street is the quintessential local coffee shop, complete with a bike mounted on the wall and a friendly resident cat. It's pretense-free and bills itself as a "community resource center" to boot. Try a lavender latte, and don't miss the guava cookies. *1532 SE Clinton St. at 16th Ave.* ☎ *503/239-8411. $.*

⑤ ★ Southeast Clinton Street. The stretch of Clinton Street from 16th to 26th avenues definitely takes the prize for cutest street ramble in this part of town. It's dotted with local shops, cafes, bars, and restaurants, from the upscale Silk Road cuisine of **Vindalho** (2038 SE Clinton St. at 20th Ave., ☎ **503/467-4550**) to the Swedish favorite **Bröder** (2508 SE Clinton St. at 25th Ave., ☎ **503/736-3333**), all without sacrificing its offbeat residential neighborhood vibe. The art-house **Clinton Street Theater** (2522 SE Clinton St. at 26th Ave., ☎ **503/238-8899**) has been showing the cult classic *The Rocky Horror Picture Show* every Saturday night since 1978, the longest run in the world. Beer lovers can even grab a pint at the tiny attached brewpub and bring it in with them. ⏱ *1 hr.*

6 People's Food Co-op. To experience Portland's fresh-local-seasonal-organic foodie mania in its purest essence—you know, the one behind all those "Know Your Farmer" bumper stickers—pop into this cooperative grocery store just south of Clinton Street. Whether it's local dairy products in glass bottles or hard-to-find bulk items like mulberries and jungle peanuts, they have it, along with prepackaged snack items, a fresh juice cart, and a year-round farmers' market every Wednesday out front. ⏱ *15 min. 3029 SE 21st Ave.* ☎ *503/674-2642. www.peoples.coop. Daily 8am–10pm.*

7 ★ Ladd's Addition. North of the Clinton neighborhood is one of the city's most distinctive residential districts, a diagonal grid extending from Division to Hawthorne streets and 12th to 20th avenues. The highlights for visitors, aside from the general serenity of the place, are the five rose gardens incorporated into the layout. A large central garden and four smaller diamond-shaped ones at the points of the compass are all meticulously tended, with more than 3,000 plants representing over 60 varieties. ⏱ *45 min. See p 23,* **5**.

8 The Hat Museum. Tucked away in the Ladd-Reingold House, one of Ladd's Addition's older homes, is this incredible collection of chapeaus, a private labor of love that's one of the largest of its kind in the country. Some 1,300 hats date back to 1845 and include hats worn in the movies *Gangs of New York* and *Chicago.* A pre-arranged tour is required, but well worth it. ⏱ *1½ hr. See p 36,* **10**.

The food cart "pod" at SE Hawthorne Street and 12th Avenue, aka **9 Cartopia,** was one of the first to really take hold in Portland, and now has covered outdoor seating and an ATM. Take your pick from Belgian-style fries or *poutine* (fries with cheese curds and gravy) at **Potato Champion** (☎ *503/505-7086*), a vegan apple pie at **Whiffies Fried Pies** (☎ *503/946-6544*), or a freshly made wood-oven pizza at **Pyro Pizza** (☎ *503/929-1404*), among others. *Hours vary, most carts open until 3am.*

10 Kidd's Toy Museum. The last stop on this tour is another private collection, this time of vintage games and toys. Owner Frank Kidd is full of stories about the items featured in the multiroom display, which includes an astonishing array of cast-iron mechanical banks and more than a few cringe-inducing examples of less PC days of yore. ⏱ *1 hr. See p 36,* **9**.

Sellwood

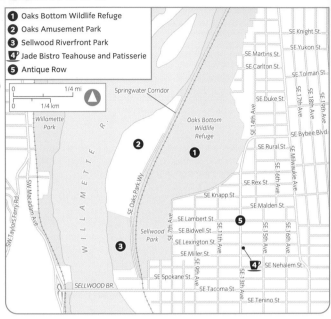

1. Oaks Bottom Wildlife Refuge
2. Oaks Amusement Park
3. Sellwood Riverfront Park
4. Jade Bistro Teahouse and Patisserie
5. Antique Row

Technically part of Portland, Sellwood feels more like a distinct village on the banks of the Willamette Valley. You don't have to take a passenger ferry here anymore like in the 19th century—you can even arrive by bike along the paved Springwater Corridor trail from OMSI (4 miles, 20–25 min). Most of Sellwood's boutiques, coffee shops, restaurants, and antiques stores are concentrated along SE Milwaukee Avenue and SE 13th Avenue. Otherwise, it's a homey neighborhood of bungalows and Victorian cottages, perfect for strolling, especially through the parks along the riverbank. **START: Bus 70.**

1 ★ Oaks Bottom Wildlife Refuge. Two trails meander through this 141-acre flood-plain wetland on the east bank of the Willamette: a hiking trail along the river bluff, and the paved Springwater Corridor linking Sellwood and Portland's East Bank Esplanade. The woodlands, pond, and meadows are home to scores of birds, including quail, hawks, ducks, woodpeckers, and kestrels. You'll find plenty of great blue herons (Portland's official city bird), since this former construction landfill is close to the Ross Island rookery. If you forgot your field guide, just look up—the huge hand-painted mural on the outside

Ferris wheel at Oaks Amusement Park.

of the Wilhelm Portland Memorial Mausoleum portrays many of the birds that call Oaks Bottom home, including a 65-foot great blue heron and a 40-foot osprey. This 43,000-square-foot mural is likely the largest of its kind in the country. ⏱ *45 min. Parking lots and trail heads at SE Milwaukee Ave. & McLoughlin Blvd., and at SE 7th Ave. & Sellwood Blvd.* ☎ *503/823-6131. Open daily 5am–midnight.*

2 ★★ kids **Oaks Amusement Park.** It's hard to decide who enjoys this old-timey amusement park more: the tots riding the carousel and miniature train, the teenagers screaming themselves hoarse on the spinning modern rides, or the parents herding everyone around. Oaks is the oldest continually operating amusement park in the country, in business since 1905, and it packs a lot into a little space on the banks of the Willamette,

from the usual—carnival games, Ferris wheel, bumper cars—to the unique, including a 1912 carved carousel and large wooden skating rink complete with pipe organ. *See p 31,* **10**.

3 **Sellwood Riverfront Park.** Just south of Oaks Bottom at the base of the close-to-crumbling Sellwood Bridge, this riverside park offers hiking trails, picnic tables, beach access, and a small wetland reserve at its north end. The open grassy part includes an off-leash area for dogs. Walk north along the riverbank a little ways for a good view of downtown Portland, and to find a bobbing enclave of cozy houseboats. Free public concerts happen on Monday evenings in the summer. On the other side of SE Oaks Park Way (and the train tracks and Springwater Corridor) is the larger **Sellwood Park,** with a swimming pool, sports fields and courts, and a playground. ⏱ *45 min. Entrance at SE Spokane St. & Oaks Pkwy. Open daily 5am–midnight.*

Sellwood Riverfront Park.

Jade Bistro Teahouse and Patisserie.

A modern take on an Asian tea-house, **4** **Jade Bistro Tea-house and Patisserie** offers a complete Vietnamese menu, but also a good selection of smaller bites such as baguette sandwiches, spicy green papaya salad, and, of course, lots and lots of teas. Desserts are a specialty, especially the Vietnamese Wedding Cake and chocolate-and-sea-salt French maca-roons. *7912 SE 13th Ave.* ☎ *503/ 477-8985. $$.*

5 **Antique Row.** If there's one thing Sellwood is known for, it's

Touring Oaks Park on the train.

antiquing. More than 50 vintage stores along SE 13th Avenue brim with furniture, housewares, jewelry, and more. It may take some digging to find your own particular treasure, of course—but that's half the fun, right? Just a few outstanding examples include **Justin & Burks** (8301 SE 13th Ave. at Umatilla St.), the **Sellwood Antique Collective** (8027 SE 13th Ave. at Spokane), **Raven Antiques and Military** (7929 SE 13th Ave. at Miller St.), and **Madison Park Antiques** (7805 SE 13th Ave. at Lambert St.). ⏱ *1 hr. Along SE 13th Ave., roughly btw. Malden & Tacoma sts.* ●

Shopping Best Bets

Best for **Books**
★★★ Powell's City of Books, *1005 W. Burnside St. (p 77)*

Best for **Shoes**
★★ Imelda's & Louie's Shoes, *935 NW Everett St. (p 80)*

Best for **Unexpected Discoveries**
★★★ Cargo, *380 NW 13th Ave. (p 81)*

Best for **Toys**
★★★ Finnegan's Toys, *922 SW Yamhill St. (p 83)*

Best for **Vintage Surprises**
★★ Ampersand Vintage, *2916 NE Alberta St. Ste. B (p 77)*

Best for **Oregon Souvenirs**
★★ Made in Oregon, *Pioneer Place Mall (p 80)*

Best for **Hats**
★★ John Helmer Haberdasher, *969 SW Broadway Ave. (p 80)*

Best for **Kids' Clothes**
★★ Hanna Andersson, *327 NW 10th Ave. (p 79)*

Best for **Jewelry**
★★★ Gilt, *720 NW 23rd Ave. (p 81)*

Best for **Sheer Selection**
★ Pioneer Place Mall, *700 SW 5th Ave. (p 82)*

Best for **Used Outfits**
★ Red Light Clothing Exchange, *3590 SE Hawthorne Blvd. (p 80)*

Best for **Records & CDs**
★★ Music Millennium, *3158 E. Burnside St. (p 82)*

Best for **Fragrances**
★ The Perfume House, *3328 SE Hawthorne Blvd. (p 78)*

Best to **Satisfy Your Inner Nerd**
★★ Things From Another World, *4133 NE Sandy Blvd. (p 77)*; and ★ Cosmic Monkey Comics, *5335 NE Sandy Blvd. (p 77)*

Best **Fresh, Local, Sustainable, Organic Produce Selection**
★★★ PSU Farmers Market, *SW Park Ave. at SW Montgomery St. (p 82)*

Below: Finnegan's Toys. Previous page: Upcycled goods at Redux.

Downtown Shopping

Augen Gallery 13
Blackfish Gallery 8
Canoe 16
Cargo 7
Clear Creek Distillery 1
Columbia Sportswear 21
CorkScru 9
Crafty Wonderland 17
Finnegan's Toys 18
Frances May 15
Gilt 3
Hanna Andersson 10
Imelda's and Louie's Shoes 11
John Helmer Haberdasher 22
Lizard Lounge 5
Macy's 26
Made in Oregon 25
Museum of Contemporary
  Craft Gallery 12
Niketown 23
Nordstrom 20
Oblation Papers & Press 6
Pioneer Place 25
Portland Pendleton Shop 24
Portland Saturday Market 27
Powell's City of Books 14
The Real Mother Goose 19
Shogun's Gallery 2
Twist 4

East Side Shopping

Amenity Shoes **4**
Ampersand Vintage **3**
Broadway Books **7**
Cosmic Monkey Comics **5**
Fourteen 30 Contemporary **10**
Grasshopper **2**
Green Bean Books **1**
Lloyd Center **8**

Mink Boutique **14**
Music Millennium **11**
Noun **12**
The Perfume House **13**
Presents of Mind **16**
Red Light Clothing Exchange **15**
Redux **9**
Things From Another World **6**

Portland Shopping A to Z

Art

★★ Ampersand Vintage
ALBERTA   Are offbeat antique images your thing? Come here for 19th-century beetle prints, botanical cyanotypes, old mug shot photographs, and more. *2916 NE Alberta St. Ste. B (at 29th Ave.).* ☎ *503/805-5458. www.ampersandvintage.com. MC, V. Bus: 72. Map p 76.*

Augen Gallery DOWNTOWN
One of Portland's older galleries shows paintings and prints by regional artists and printmakers; their Pearl gallery (817 SW 2nd Ave.); ☎ 503/224-8182) specializes in prints. *716 NW Davis St. (at 7th Ave.).* ☎ *503/546-5056. www.augengallery.com. MC, V. Bus: 15 or 51. Map p 75.*

★★ Blackfish Gallery PEARL
This artist-owned cooperative isn't afraid to push the envelope, showing contemporary images as well as mixed-media pieces by lesser-known artists. *420 NW 9th Ave. (at Flanders St.).* ☎ *503/224-2634. www.blackfish.com. MC, V. Streetcar: NW 10th & Glisan; bus: 17. Map p 75.*

★ Fourteen 30 Contemporary
SOUTHEAST   Step inside this immaculate white space to find works by artists on the cusp of breaking big. Often shows video and sculpture, too, unusual for Portland. *922 SE Ankeny St. at 10th Ave.* ☎ *503/236-1430. www.fourteen30.com. MC, V. Bus: 12, 19, 20, or 70. Map p 76.*

Books, Magazines & Comics

Broadway Books NORTHEAST
At this quintessential neighborhood bookstore, the owners have an excellent eye for titles and are happy to point you to just the right book. *1714 NE Broadway Ave. (at 17th St.).* ☎ *503/284-1726. www.broadwaybooks.net. AE, MC, V. Bus: 9 or 77. Map p 76.*

★★ Cosmic Monkey Comics
NORTHEAST   No matter what you're after—anime, manga, graphic novels, or the latest titles—you'll find it here at Portland's premier comics store. Don't miss the back room, full of back issues and trades. *5335 NE Sandy Blvd. (at Sandycrest Terrace).* ☎ *503/517-9050. www.cosmicmonkeycomics.com. AE, MC, V. Bus: 12. Map p 76.*

★ Green Bean Books ALBERTA
Imagine the ideal children's bookstore: new and used books in a colorful space, comfy couches, and even a draping bush tree out back to read under. That's Green Bean Books. *1600 NE Alberta St. (at 16th Ave.).* ☎ *503/954-2354. www.greenbeanbookspdx.com. AE, MC, V. Bus: 72. Map p 76.*

★★★ Powell's City of Books
PEARL   What can you say about the world's best independent bookstore, a full city block of literature? Don't visit Portland without popping in at Powell's. *1005 W. Burnside St. (at 10th Ave.).* ☎ *503/228-4651. www.powells.com. AE, MC, V. Bus: 20; Streetcar: NW 10th & Couch. Map p 75.*

★★ Things From Another World HOLLYWOOD   Fanboys rejoice! Not just wall-to-wall comics, but also collectible toys, figurines, games, and a couch for perusing. *4133 NE Sandy Blvd. (at 44th Ave.).* ☎ *503/284-4693. www.tfaw.com. MC, V. Bus: 12. Map p 76.*

Crafty Wonderland.

Cosmetics & Perfumes

★ **The Perfume House** HAWTHORNE Everyone needs his or her own scent, right? Owner Chris Tsefalas, one of only 26 official "Noses" in the world, will help you discover your own special fragrance. *3328 SE Hawthorne Blvd. (at 33rd Ave.).* ☎ *503/234-5375. www.the perfumehouse.com. MC, V. Bus: 14. Map p 76.*

Crafts

★ **Crafty Wonderland** DOWNTOWN What started as a temporary "pop-up shop" is now a permanent home to works by more than 90 talented local artisans,

stocking cards, clothing, soap, pins, and much, much more. *802 SW 10th Ave. (at Yamhill St.).* ☎ *503/224-9097. www.craftywonderland.com/pop-up-shop. MC, V. Streetcar: Central Library. Map p 75.*

Museum of Contemporary Craft Gallery PEARL The small retail gallery of this venerable museum sells jewelry and works made of ceramic, glass, fiber, metal, and wood, with prices toward the high end. *724 NW Davis St. (at 8th Ave.).* ☎ *503/223-2654. www.museumofcontemporarycraft.org. MC, V. Bus: 9 or 17. Map p 75.*

★★ **Portland Saturday Market** OLDTOWN/CHINATOWN Every Saturday *and* Sunday from March through December, some 300 artists set up shop outdoors under the west end of the Burnside Bridge. Free entertainment and food round out the fun. *W. Burnside Ave. btw. SW 1st Ave. & SW Naito Pkwy.* ☎ *503/222-6072. www.portland saturdaymarket.com. MAX: Skidmore Fountain; bus: 16. Map p 75.*

★ **The Real Mother Goose** DOWNTOWN If "unique" is your favorite shopping adjective, come to Portland's top crafts shop for one-of-a-kind jewelry, carved wood,

Browsing the Saturday Market.

The decidedly upscale Frances May.

blown glass, textiles, and accessories. *901 SW Yamhill St.* ☎ *503/223-9510. www.therealmothergoose.com. Also at Portland International Airport, Main Terminal (*☎ *503/284-9929). AE, MC, V. MAX: Library/SW 9th Ave. Map p 75.*

Twist NORTHWEST True to its name, this boutique gallery carries creative housewares and handmade jewelry, and everything is just a little bit out of the ordinary—in a good way. *30 NW 23rd Place (at Westover Rd.).* ☎ *503/224-0334. www.twistonline.com. Also at Pioneer Place Shopping Center, 700 SW 5th Ave. (*☎ *503/222-3137). AE, MC, V. Bus: 15 or 18. Map p 75.*

Department Stores

Macy's DOWNTOWN The first six floors of the historic Meier & Frank building near Pioneer Courthouse Square are stuffed with clothes, accessories, housewares, makeup, and more. *621 SW 5th Ave.* ☎ *503/223-0512. www.macys.com. Also at 1001 Lloyd Center (*☎ *503/281-4797). AE, MC, V. MAX: Pioneer Courthouse/SW 6th Ave.; bus: 1, 8, 12, or 94. Map p 75.*

Nordstrom DOWNTOWN Another national department store on Pioneer Square, Nordstrom offers a more intimate experience than Macy's. For deals, try nearby **Nordstrom Rack** (245 SW Morrison St.). *701 SW Broadway Ave. (at Morrison St.).* ☎ *503/224-6666. www.nordstrom.com. Also at 1001 Lloyd Center (*☎ *503/287-2444). AE, MC, V. MAX: Pioneer Square North. Map p 75.*

Fashion

Amenity Shoes NORTHEAST Chic shoes (for both sexes) and bags in the Beaumont-Wilshire neighborhood. Many unique styles. *3430 NE 41st Ave. (at Fremont St.).* ☎ *503/282-4555. www.amenityshoes.com. MC, V. Bus: 24 or 75. Map p 76.*

Columbia Sportswear DOWNTOWN This local sportswear giant's flagship store brims with rugged but tasteful gear, housed in what looks like a giant log cabin. Prices are lower at the factory outlet in Sellwood (1323 SE Tacoma St., ☎ 503/238-0118). *911 SW Broadway Ave. (at Taylor St.).* ☎ *503/226-6800. www.columbia.com. AE, MC, V. MAX: Library/SW 9th Ave.; bus: 15 or 51. Map p 75.*

★ **Frances May** DOWNTOWN Quite possibly the city's top women's boutique, with high-end brands befitting New York or Los Angeles. *1013 SW Washington St. (at 10th Ave.).* ☎ *503/227-3402. www.francesmay.com. AE, MC, V. Streetcar: SW 10th & Stark; bus: 15 or 51. Map p 75.*

★★ **Hanna Andersson** PEARL Children's clothes get a sunny Swedish makeover. This place is like catnip to grandparents, but the kids love it too. And there's a cupcake shop down the block! *327 NW 10th Ave. (at Flanders St.).* ☎ *503/321-5275. www.hannaanderson.com. AE, MC, V. MAX: NW 11th & Everett; bus: 17. Map p 75.*

★★ Imelda's and Louie's Shoes
NORTHWEST Boots, high heels, Mary Janes: If they're stylish and go on your feet, they have 'em here, even though you might have to save up. The east-side branch (3426 SE Hawthorne Blvd.; ☎ 503/233-7476) has less attitude. *935 NW Everett St. (at 10th Ave.).* ☎ *503/595-4970. www.imeldasandlouies.com. MC, V. MAX: NW 10th & Everett. Map p 75.*

★★ John Helmer Haberdasher
DOWNTOWN Hankering for a hat? Craving a chapeau? John Helmer has been selling everything from fezzes to fedoras since 1921. *969 SW Broadway Ave. (at Salmon St.).* ☎ *503/223-4976. www.johnhelmer.com. MC, V. Bus: 15 or 51. Map p 75.*

Lizard Lounge
PEARL Hip duds for men and women, including sustainable local brand Nau and national ones like Billabong and Ray-Ban. And a Ping-Pong table. *1323 NW Irving St. (at 14th Ave.).* ☎ *503/416-7476. www.lizardloungepdx.com. MC, V. Bus: 17. Map p 75.*

★ Mink Boutique
SOUTHEAST Adorable dresses, sassy skirts, and fit-like-a-glove jeans—plus a friendly, knowledgeable sales staff—make this a neighborhood favorite. *3418 SE Hawthorne Blvd. (at 34th Ave.).* ☎ *503/232-3500. www.shopmink.com. MC, V. Bus: 14. Map p 76.*

Niketown
DOWNTOWN A temple to athletic performance (and the clothing thereof); fitting since Nike got its start here. The outlet (2650 NE Martin Luther King Jr. Blvd., ☎ 503/281-5901) has deals on last year's lines. *930 SW 6th Ave. (at Salmon St.).* ☎ *503/221-6453. www.nike.com. AE, MC, V. Bus: 35, 36, 44, 54, 56, or 99. Map p 75.*

Portland Pendleton Shop
DOWNTOWN Outfit yourself against the damp chill with fine wool fashions from this Northwest institution, and grab one of their famous blankets for home. *900 SW 5th Ave. (at Taylor St.).* ☎ *503/242-0037. www.pendleton-usa.com. AE, MC, V. MAX: NW 6th & Davis sts.; bus: 9 or 17. Map p 75.*

★ Red Light Clothing Exchange
SOUTHEAST Vintage clothes are de rigeur to a certain stripe of Portlander, and this place has one of the biggest selections in town. *3590 SE Hawthorne Blvd. (at 36th Ave.).* ☎ *503/963-8888. www.redlightclothingexchange.com. MC, V. Bus: 14. Map p 76.*

Gifts & Souvenirs

★★ Made in Oregon
The full bounty of the Beaver State in one place—Tillamook cheese, Pendleton blankets, Timbers jerseys, Willamette pinots—make this the go-to place for local gifts. *Pioneer Place Mall, 340 SW Morrison St.* ☎ *503/241-3630. Also in the airport (☎ 503/282-7827); and in Lloyd Center Mall, 1017 Lloyd Center (☎ 503/282-7636). www.madeinoregon.com. AE, MC, V. Map p 75.*

Presents of Mind
SOUTHEAST Locally made jewelry, witty cards, and offbeat gifts make this an

Quirky must-haves at Presents of Mind.

Cargo's eclectic Asiana.

all-in-one gift-shopping destination. *3633 SE Hawthorne Blvd. (at 36th Ave.).* ☎ *503/230-7740. www. presentsofmind.tv. AE, MC, V. Bus: 14. Map p 76.*

Housewares

★ **Canoe** DOWNTOWN   On the west end of downtown, this modern home store is great for thoughtful gifts for men and women, from kitchen items to cast-iron bottle openers from Japan. *1136 SW Alder St. (at 12th Ave.).* ☎ *503/889-8545. www.canoeonline.net. AE, MC, V. Streetcar: SW 11th & Alder; bus: 15 or 51. Map p 75.*

★★★ **Cargo** PEARL   You'll feel like you've stumbled into a Chinese warehouse during a festival at this kaleidoscopic place, full of furniture, Asian antiques, paper lanterns, jewelry, and other sundries. *380 NW 13th Ave. (at Flanders St.).* ☎ *503/ 209-8349. www.cargoinc.com. MC, V. MAX: NW 11th & Everett; bus: 17. Map p 75.*

★★ **Noun** SOUTHEAST   Cleverly subtitled "A Person's Place for Things," this east-side nook carries charming antiques, artisan jewelry, and handmade stationery—plus you enter through a cupcake shop. *3300*

SE Belmont St. (at 33rd Ave.). ☎ *503/235-0078. www.shopnoun. com. MC, V. Bus: 15. Map p 76.*

Shogun's Gallery NORTHWEST All things Asian, including Chinese and Japanese furniture, ceramics, bronze lanterns, and prints. *1111 NW 23rd Ave. (at Marshall St.).* ☎ *503/ 224-0328. www.shogunsgallery.com. MC, V. Streetcar: NW 23rd & Marshall; bus: 15. Map p 75.*

Jewelry & Accessories

★★★ **Gilt** NORTHWEST   A perennial favorite for its vintage and locally designed jewelry, including many one-of-a-kind items. It's hard to leave empty-handed. *720 NW 23rd Ave. (at Johnson St.).* ☎ *503/ 226-0629. www.giltjewelry.com. AE, MC, V. Bus: 15. Map p 75.*

★★ **Redux** SOUTHEAST   Everything in here used to be something else—all the wallets, belt buckles, ties, and jewelry are made of repurposed materials, often to charming and creative effect. *811 E. Burnside St. #110.* ☎ *503/231-7336. www. reduxpdx.com. MC, V. Bus: 12, 19, or 20. Map p 76.*

Hypnotic treasures and trinkets at Gilt.

Reduce, Reuse, Redux.

Malls & Markets

Lloyd Center NORTHEAST The biggest shopping complex in the state could use some updating, but it does have 200 stores, a full movie theater, and even an indoor ice rink. *Btw. NE Multnomah & NE Halsey sts., from 9th to 13th aves.* ☎ *503/282-2511. www.lloydcenter.com. MAX: Lloyd Center/NE 11th Ave.; bus: 8, 9, 70, 73, or 77. Map p 76.*

★ **Pioneer Place** DOWNTOWN The most fashionable shopping center in downtown, Pioneer Place has

Vendors at PSU Farmers Market.

everything from an Apple store to Victoria's Secret, plus a Regal cinema and a food court. *700 SW 5th Ave. (at Morrison St.).* ☎ *503/228-5800. www.pioneerplace.com. MAX: Mall/SW 4th Ave.; bus: 1, 8, 12, or 94. Map p 75.*

★★★ **PSU Farmers Market** DOWNTOWN The biggest and by far most popular of Portland's six seasonal open-air markets, the one at PSU fills 2 full park blocks with fresh-off-the-farm produce, flowers, cheese, wine, meat, seafood, and other goodies. *SW Park Ave. at SW Montgomery St.* ☎ *503/241-0032. www.portlandfarmersmarket.org. Free admission. Streetcar: SW Park & Mill. Map p 75.*

Music/CDs

★★ **Music Millennium** LAURELHURST Think of it as the musical equivalent of Powell's Books: a vast library of new and used, some rare treasures, plus in-store performances by top artists. *3158 E. Burnside St. (at 32nd Ave.).* ☎ *503/231-8926. www.musicmillennium.com. MC, V. Bus: 20. Map p 76.*

Stationery & Cards
★ Oblation Papers & Press

PEARL   Unique, high-quality stationery, cards, wedding invites, and the like made on handmade paper with century-old letterpresses. *516 NW 12th Ave. (at Hoyt St.).* ☎ *503/223-1093. www.oblationpapers.com. MC, V. Streetcar: NW 11th & Glisan. Map p 75.*

Toys & Novelties
★★★ Finnegan's Toys

DOWNTOWN   This über-toystore is fun for adults, let alone kids, with an emphasis on learning and quality over buzzers and blinking lights. *922 SW Yamhill St. (at 10th Ave.).* ☎ *503/221-0306. www.finnegans toys.com. AE, MC, V. Streetcar: Central Library; MAX: Library/SW 9th Ave. Map p 75.*

★ Grasshopper

ALBERTA   Handmade children's clothes, European toys, and award-winning books—this place is enough to make you want kids if you don't have them already. *1816 NE Alberta St. (at 18th Ave.).* ☎ *503/335-3131. www. grasshopperstore.com. MC, V. Bus: 72. Map p 76.*

The unofficial city motto.

Miles of music at Music Millennium.

Wines & Spirits
Clear Creek Distillery

NORTHWEST   Combine European brandy-making techniques with Oregon fruit and you get unbeatable eaux de vie, grappa, wine brandy, and fruit liqueurs, all of which you can sample here. *2389 NW Wilson St. (at 24th Ave.).* ☎ *503/248-9470. www.clear creekdistillery.com. MC, V. Bus: 15, 17, or 77. Map p 75.*

CorkScru

PEARL   These guys know their vintages, especially sub-$12 values, and they specialize in

Wine brandy at Clear Creek Distillery.

wine six-packs from Italy, France, and, of course, Oregon. *339 NW Broadway (at Flanders St.).*

☎ *503/226-9463. www.corkscru.biz. MC, V. Bus: 9 or 17. Map p 75.* ●

Farmers Markets

The Portland metro area supports no fewer than six seasonal open-air farmers markets (www.portlandfarmersmarket.org). Along with farm-fresh produce and meats, you'll often find food carts, live music, crafts, and more.

- **Pioneer Courthouse Square Market:** SW Broadway & SW Morrison Street, Mondays June–September 10am–2pm; Tuesdays and Thursdays, July–August, 11am–2pm.
- **Shemanski Park Market:** SW Park Avenue at SW Salmon Street, Wednesdays May–October, 10am–2pm.
- **Winter Market at Shemanski Park:** SW Park Avenue at SW Salmon Street, Saturdays January 7–February 25, 10am–2pm.
- **Northwest Market:** NW 19th Avenue at NW Everett Street, Thursdays June–September, 3–7pm.
- **Buckman Market:** SE Salmon Street at 20th Avenue, Thursdays May–September, 3–7pm.
- **Portland State University Market:** Saturdays March–December, 8:30am–2pm.
- **King Market:** NE 7th Avenue at NE Wygant Street, 10am–2pm, Sundays May–October, 10am–2pm.

Forest **Park**

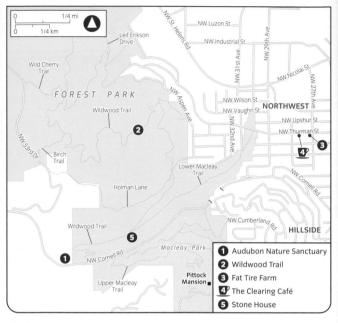

1 Audubon Nature Sanctuary
2 Wildwood Trail
3 Fat Tire Farm
4 The Clearing Café
5 Stone House

Extending 8 miles from the heart of Portland, **Forest Park points** like a lush green finger toward the mouth of the Columbia. At 5,100 acres, it's the U.S.'s largest natural forested area within city limits, with 8 square miles of fern-filled ravines, rushing streams, and towering firs, cedars, maples, and alders. The city's green playground is spiderwebbed with more than 80 miles of trails and fire lanes for hiking, biking, and trail-running, and is home to over 112 bird and 62 mammal species. There's no visitor center or main entrance; instead, at least 17 access points circle the park edge. (One main gateway is the start of Leif Erikson Drive, a 12-mile gravel road, at the end of NW Thurman St.) The west end of the park, away from downtown, is much wilder than the more heavily visited eastern end. **START: Drive to 5151 NW Cornell Rd.**

---

1 **kids** ★ **Audubon Nature Sanctuary.** Tucked up against Forest Park's southern side, this wildlife rehabilitation center is home to all

kinds of injured critters being nursed back to health (or who were simply given a place to live), from vultures to bald eagles. Sometimes

Previous page: Alternative cycling on Mt Tabor.

Exploring Forest Park

they'll bring the animals out for up close encounters. There's a gift shop and 150 acres of forest with a few miles of trails, including a newt-filled pond. It's also a good starting point for the Wildwood and Upper MacLeay trails in Forest Park itself next door. *See p 21,* ➋.

➋ ★★ **Wildwood Trail.** Forest Park's longest trail is 27 sinuous miles of fern-lined curves, stream crossings, and switchbacks (plus another three in Washington Park). This National Recreation Trail is marked by blue diamonds and mile markers every quarter mile, which make it easy to take it in pieces; almost every loop hike in the park involves the Wildwood. Its eastern end sees a good bit of foot traffic, while its west end is in the wilder western part of the park.

➌ **Fat Tire Farm.** Close to 30 miles of fire roads in Forest Park are open to mountain bikers. (Hiking trails, though, are not.) To try a few out, head to this bike shop 1 mile down Thurman Street from the Leif

Erickson Drive entrance, and rent a high-end mountain bike for the day. ⏱ *30 min. 2714 NW Thurman St. (at 27th Ave.).* ☎ *503/222-3276. www.fattirefarm.com. Bikes are $40–$125 for 24 hr. Mon–Fri 11am–7pm; Sat 10am–6pm; Sun noon–5pm.*

Fuel up for your hike (or recover afterward) with the healthy soups, panini, and tasty rice-and-bean bowls at ➍ **The Clearing Café** downhill from the Leif Erikson Drive entrance. *2772 NW Thurman St. (at 27th Ave.).* ☎ *503/841-6240. $.*

➎ **Stone House.** This old restroom near Balch Creek, built by the Works Progress Administration in 1936, has grown evocatively moss-covered and roofless over the decades. It's a good place to take a break and ogle the park's largest tree: a 242-foot Douglas fir with a trunk 17.3 feet in diameter. Reach it via the easy 1-mile Lower Macleay Trail from Lower Macleay Park (NW Upshur St. entrance). ⏱ *90 min.*

Washington **Park**

1. Hoyt Arboretum
2. Vietnam Veterans of Oregon Memorial
3. World Forestry Discovery Center Museum
4. Portland Children's Museum
5. Oregon Zoo
6. Elephants Deli
7. Japanese Garden
8. International Rose Test Garden
9. Pittock Mansion

Forest Park's more urbane neighbor covers 410 acres of wooded hills between West Burnside Street and U.S. 26. It's basically an extension of the same steep forests, albeit with more developed attractions in a smaller space. Cougars don't roam the woods any more like they did in the 19th century, but plenty of dogs do, with their jogging owners in tow, on the park's 15-plus miles of trails. A shuttle bus runs from the Washington Park MAX station (the deepest transit station in North America, at 260 feet down) to the Japanese and rose gardens and the arboretum (daily June–Sept, and on weekends in May and Oct). START: MAX Washington Park; Bus 63 on weekdays only.

1 ★ **Hoyt Arboretum.** This 187-acre reserve is much more than a woodsy park—it's a living museum of plants, with more than 8,000 shrubs and trees representing over 1,000 species from around the world. Dozens of these are endangered in the wild, and they're all organized according to where they came from and how they're related. There's always something in season, from fiery fall colors and the scents of spring to summer wildflowers and the mellow colors of the special Winter Garden. Twelve miles of hiking trails wind through the place, including the Wildwood Trail that continues into Forest Park. Pick up

Hoyt Arboretum.

③ kids World Forestry Discovery Center Museum. The timber industry's major role in the development of the Pacific Northwest is the focus of this interactive museum geared mostly toward kids. Learn about the creatures who live under the forest floor, and ride into the (simulated) canopy of the Amazon rainforest. Out front sits "Peggy," a 33.5-ton locomotive built in 1909, who hauled a billion feet of logs, more or less, in her 41-year career. *See p 22, ③*.

④ ★★ kids Portland Children's Museum. Are the tykes tired of trees? The Children's Museum isn't huge, but it packs a lot into a modest space: a treehouse for story time, a studio for making art from recycled materials, a miniature grocery store complete with shopping carts and scanners. Kids 8 and under or so will love this place, often pleading for repeat visits to try it all. Traveling

maps for suggested routes of 1, 2, or 4 miles, or go on a 90-minute guided tour offered on Saturdays in the summer and fall. 🕑 *90 min. 4000 SW Fairview Blvd.* ☎ *503/865-8733. Free admission; guided tours $3 per person, most Sat late June–Sept. Visitor center open Mon–Fri 9am–4pm; Sat 9am–3pm. Grounds open 6am–10pm daily. MAX: Washington Park. Bus: 63 on weekdays only.*

② Vietnam Veterans of Oregon Memorial. On the south edge of the arboretum, this monument centers on a curved wall of black granite listing the names of Oregonians who died or went missing in action in Vietnam, echoing the more famous memorial in Washington, D.C. A spiral path leads past smaller walls with narratives from the conflict contrasted with local events. *4000 SW Canyon Rd. Open daily 5am–10pm. MAX: Washington Park. Bus: 63 on weekdays only.*

Among the many trails at Hoyt.

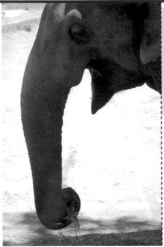

A local at the Oregon Zoo.

exhibits, classes, and visiting artists, musicians, and storytellers mean there's always something new on. *See p 27,* **2**.

5 ★★ **kids Oregon Zoo.** Completing the child-friendly trifecta at the southern end of Washington Park, Portland's zoo began with two bears—a grizzly named Grace and a brown bear named Brownie—in the 1880s—and snowballed from there. Now it's the most popular paid attraction in the state, with 64 acres of felines, canines, primates, and pachyderms. Successful breeding programs for Asian elephants and California condors are the backbone of their conservation efforts. Two seasonal events pack in even more visitors: a summer evening open-air concert series and a winter holiday light show, best viewed from the 5/6-scale steam train that chugs as far as the Japanese and Rose Test gardens. *See p 15,* **2**.

No relation to the zoo, the **6 Elephants Deli** just outside the park has wood-fired pizza, grilled sandwiches, and a sorely tempting dessert case. Try the garlic fries or a salad from the cold case. *115 NW 22nd Ave. (at Davis St.).* ☎ *503/299-6304. $$.*

7 ★★★ **Japanese Garden.** Near the top of Portland's must-see list is this tranquil oasis of gravel paths, koi ponds, and painstakingly manicured trees. It's the closest you can come to visiting Japan without hopping on a plane; in fact, it's said to be the most authentic Japanese garden outside of the country itself. Plus, the views of Mount Hood from the Pavilion are outstanding. *See p 15,* **1**.

8 ★★ **International Rose Test Garden.** Portland's floral showpiece was conceived in the chaos of WWI, when local rose hobbyists feared the bombs raining down on Europe might snuff out entire breeds. Today it's home to about 10,000 blooming bushes, with a focus on new hybrids. How pretty is this place? Put it this way: Every January first, even before the gardens open, there's already a line of couples outside applying for permits to have their weddings here. Kids may not be thrilled by rows upon rows of flowers, but just down SW Kingston Avenue is the **Rose Garden Children's Park,** a sprawling playground next to a picnic shelter in the zoo's old elephant barn. *See p 13,* **10**.

9 ★★ **Pittock Mansion.** While not technically in Washington Park, the mansion owned by Portland pioneer Henry Pittock is just across West

Pittock Mansion.

Burnside Avenue (be careful crossing!) via the Wildwood Trail and well worth a detour. Henry and his wife Georgiana, both first-generation Oregon immigrants, built this 23-room home in 1914 and lived in it until they died. Perched 1,000 feet above the city, the house incorporates English, French, and Turkish designs, but was built by Oregon craftsmen using Northwest materials. You can tour the interior or just enjoy the grounds, gardens, and views of Mt. Hood—first climbed by Pittock and four friends in 1854. *See p 12,* **9**.

A Rose City by Any Other Name?

Portland can thank Leo Samuel, founder of Standard Insurance, for its flowery nickname. Samuel, who lived here in the late 19th century, was such an enthusiastic rose gardener that he would leave clippers by his bushes so people could help themselves to blossoms. Other gardeners followed suit, and word soon spread that the damp city on the Willamette was a hotbed for the temperamental flowers. They're still grown outside the Standard Insurance Company's home office on SW 6th Avenue between Salmon and Taylor streets downtown. ("Stumptown," Portland's other nickname, comes from—you guessed it—the logging industry.)

Portland **by Bike**

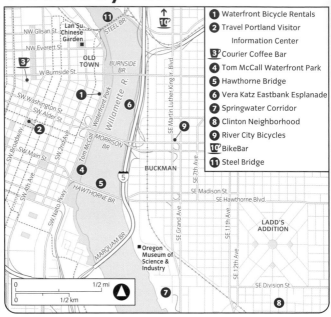

1 Waterfront Bicycle Rentals
2 Travel Portland Visitor Information Center
3 Courier Coffee Bar
4 Tom McCall Waterfront Park
5 Hawthorne Bridge
6 Vera Katz Eastbank Esplanade
7 Springwater Corridor
8 Clinton Neighborhood
9 River City Bicycles
10 BikeBar
11 Steel Bridge

It's official: **Portland is the most bike-crazy city** in the country, with the highest percentage of cycling commuters (around 7%), some 315 miles of bikeways and tons of annual events, including the two-week Pedalpalooza every June. At last count the city boasted 56 bike repair shops, 33 artisan bike builders, and 15 bike clothing manufacturers. This rolling tour offers a taste of what cycling in the City of Roses is all about. (**A word of caution:** Even though local motorists are used to driving around cyclists, and a surprising number of riders don't wear helmets, you should always wear one.) START: **MAX Oak/SW 1st Ave; Bus 16.**

1 **Waterfront Bicycle Rentals.** Didn't bring your own wheels? Don't worry—they have you covered here, with hybrid city-ready bikes for rent, as well as kids' models, tandems, child trailers, and car bike racks. All rentals include a helmet, lock, map, and light. ⏱ *30 min. 10 SW Ash St. #100 (at Naito Pkwy.).*

☎ *503/227-1719. www.waterfrontbikes.com. Daily 10am–6pm. Rentals $9/hr., $28/half-day, $40/24 hr., $100/week.*

2 **Travel Portland Visitor Information Center.** If you did bring your own bike, or if you just need a little more guidance (and a

super-handy *Bike There!* map), head to Pioneer Courthouse Square for some in-person riding advice. Odds are, whoever's behind the counter got there on two wheels him- or herself that morning. 🕐 *30 min. 701 SW 6th Ave., Pioneer Courthouse Square.* ☎ *503/275-8355. www. travelportland.com. Mon–Fri 8:30am–5:30pm; Sat 10am–4pm; Sun May–Oct 10am–2pm.*

...

Time for some leg gasoline—sorry, caffeine—at this fittingly cycle-centric little coffee roaster and cafe, **3 Courier Coffee Bar.** (They deliver their beans all over town–by bike, of course.) *923 SW Oak (at Hawthorne).* ☎ *503/545-6444. $.*

4 ★★ Tom McCall Waterfront Park. If you only ride one place in town, it should be through this skinny park along the Willamette, which makes a great start for longer rides as well. Stretching from the Steel Bridge almost to the Marquam

Burnside Bridge.

...

Fountains along the river.

(I-5) bridge, it passes fountains, cherry trees, the Saturday Market, and the 1947 stern-wheeler Portland (now home to a nautical museum). It's also one segment of a popular 3-mile loop that crosses the Steel and Hawthorne bridges to the Eastbank Esplanade (see below). *See p 11,* **6**.

5 ★ Hawthorne Bridge. Cross the river on the country's oldest vertical-lift bridge, opened in 1910 and made bike-friendly in 1999 with wide sidewalks on both sides. Now it's Oregon's busiest bicycle bridge, with some 5,000 riders rolling across every day. 🕐 *30 min.*

6 ★★ kids Vera Katz Eastbank Esplanade. Opened in 2001, this 1.5-mile bike and walking trail links the Steel and Hawthorne bridges on the east bank of the Willamette. It crosses a 1,200-foot floating walkway under the Burnside Bridge and is one of the best places to see Portland's skyline in all its riparian glory. *See p 67,* **1**.

7 ★ kids Springwater Corridor. Once a railroad that hauled passengers and produce, this 21-mile paved trail leads south from the Hawthorne Bridge and OMSI to the Sellwood neighborhood, home to Oaks Bottom Wildlife Refuge and Oaks Amusement Park. It's 4 miles

Portland by Bike

to Sellwood, a scenic out-and-back ride along the river. From there, the trail turns east as part of the 40-mile loop around most of Portland (www.40mileloop.org). *See p 68,* **3**.

8 ★ **Clinton Neighborhood.** After a detour down the Springwater Corridor and back, head east to this quintessential cycling neighborhood along SE Clinton Street and its popular bike path. There are dozens of places to eat, drink, and shop, concentrated around SE 21st and 26th avenues and at the "Seven Corners" intersection of SE Division Street and SE 20th Avenue. Look for the huge wheel of the penny-farthing outside **A Better Cycle** (2324 SE Division St., ☎ **503/265-8595**), a worker-owned bike shop. *See p 68,* **5**.

9 **River City Bicycles.** A repeat contender for Portland's best bike shop, River City is stocked literally to the rafters with bikes and gear—look for the historic models hanging from the ceiling. Staffed by friendly, erudite employees, they have a free espresso bar and an indoor test track upstairs for rainy-day test drives. For less expensive models, try their **outlet** at 534 SE Belmont St. (at 6th Ave., ☎ **503/446-2205**). *30 min. 706 SE M.L. King Blvd. (at Morrison St.). ☎ 503/233-5973. www.rivercitybicycles.com.*

Take the Esplanade, N. Interstate Avenue, and N. Williams Avenue past the Rose Garden to reach **10** **BikeBar,** the cycle-themed brewpub decorated with bike frames. Enjoy a giant pretzel and a pint from Hopworks Urban Brewery on the back patio—you earned it. *3947 N. Williams St. at Failing St. ☎ 503/237-6258. $.*

11 ★ **Steel Bridge.** Complete your tour by returning downtown via the most eye-catching of Portland's four bike-friendly bridges. (The other two are the Broadway and Burnside bridges.) Riders and pedestrians take a 220-foot cantilevered walkway suspended over the river, added on the south side in 2001. *See p 17,* **6**. ●

Let's Roll

If you'd like to explore more of the city, the Portland Bureau of Transportation offers free guided bike rides on Tuesday and Wednesday evenings at 6pm in the summer, arranged around themes like public art and nature. The Tuesday rides start at Unthank Park (N. Failing St. at N. Commercial Ave.), and Wednesday rides start at Wellington Park (NE Mason St. at 67th Ave.). ☎ *503/823-5185, www.portlandonline.com/transportation.*

6 The Best **Dining**

Dining Best Bets

Best for **Romance**
★ Chameleon, $$$ *2000 NE 40th Ave. (p 101)*

Best **Brunch**
★ Tin Shed, $ *1438 NE Alberta St. (p 109)*

Best for **Vegetarians**
★ Prasad, $ *925 NW Davis St. (p 107)*

Best for **Gourmet Carnivores**
★★ Beast, $$$ *5425 NE 30th Ave. (p 100)*

Best **Dinner Entertainment**
★ Marrakesh, $$ *1201 SW 21st Ave. (p 105)*

Best **Pizza**
★ Apizza Scholls, $$ *4741 SE Hawthorne Blvd. (p 100)*; and
★ Ken's Artisan Pizza, $$ *304 SE 28th Ave. (p 104)*

Best **Dim Sum**
★ Wong's King Seafood Restaurant, $$ *8733 SE Division St. (p 110)*

Best **Tapas**
★★★ Toro Bravo, $$ *120 NE Russell St. (p 109)*

Best **Italian**
★★★ Genoa, $$$$ *2832 SE Belmont St. (p 103)*

Best **Desserts**
★ Papa Haydn, $$$ *701 NW 23rd Ave. (p 106)*

Best **Burger**
★★ Yakuza Lounge, $$ *5411 NE 30th Ave. (p 110)*

Best **Cheap Eats**
★ Built to Grill, $ *232 SW Washington Ave. (p 101)*

Best **Happy Hour**
★ Saucebox, $$ *214 SW Broadway Ave. (p 108)*

Best **Pan-Asian**
★★ Pok Pok, $$ *3226 SE Division St. (p 107)*

Previous page: Al Fresco at 50 Plates.

Downtown Dining

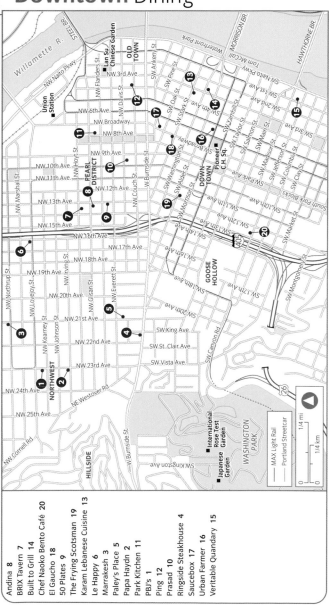

East Side Dining

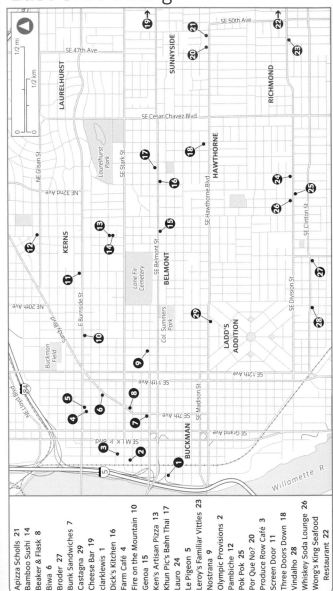

Apizza Scholls 21
Bamboo Sushi 14
Beaker & Flask 8
Biwa 6
Broder 27
Bunk Sandwiches 7
Castagna 29
Cheese Bar 19
clarklewis 1
Dick's Kitchen 16
Farm Café 4
Fire on the Mountain 10
Genoa 15
Ken's Artisan Pizza 13
Khun Pic's Bahn Thai 17
Lauro 24
Le Pigeon 5
Leroy's Familiar Vittles 23
Nostrana 9
Olympic Provisions 2
Pambiche 12
Pok Pok 25
Por Que No? 20
Produce Row Café 3
Screen Door 11
Three Doors Down 18
Vindalho 28
Whiskey Soda Lounge 26
Wong's King Seafood Restaurant 22

Northeast Dining

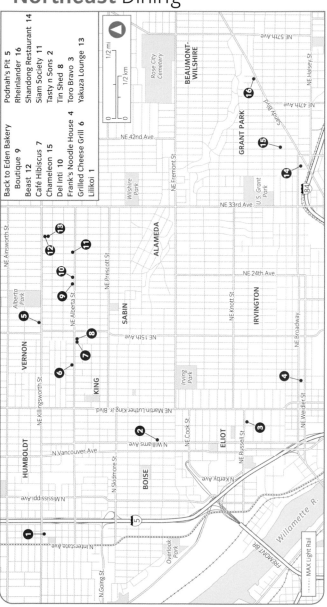

Back to Eden Bakery
Boutique **9**
Beast **12**
Café Hibiscus **7**
Chameleon **15**
Del Inti **10**
Frank's Noodle House **4**
Grilled Cheese Grill **6**
Lilikoi **1**

Podnah's Pit **5**
Rheinlander **16**
Shandong Restaurant **14**
Siam Society **11**
Tasty n Sons **2**
Tin Shed **8**
Toro Bravo **3**
Yakuza Lounge **13**

Dining **A to Z**

★★★ Andina PEARL *PERUVIAN* You've never had *nuevo andino* cuisine like this: stuffed piquillo peppers, house-made seviche, squash stew. Many plates sized to share. *1314 NW Glisan St. (at 13th Ave.).* ☎ *503/228-95350. www.andina restaurant.com. Entrees $19–30; small plates $9 and up. AE, MC, V. Lunch & dinner daily. Bus: 17. Map p 97.*

★ Apizza Scholls HAWTHORNE *PIZZA* Get in line early for some of Portland's best pizza—think hot truffle oil, goathorn peppers, and cured pork shoulder—and hope they don't run out of homemade dough, which does happen. *4741 SE Hawthorne Blvd. (at 48th Ave.).* ☎ *503/233-128550. www.apizza scholls.com. Pizzas $19–$25. AE, MC, V. Dinner daily. Bus: 14. Map p 98.*

Back to Eden Bakery Boutique ALBERTA *BAKERY* Vegan cookies, cakes, pies, and other goodies using mostly local, organic ingredients. Try a green tea whoopee pie. *2217 NE Alberta St. (at 23rd Ave.).* ☎ *503/ 477-5022. www.backtoedenbakery. com. Entrees $3–$8. MC, V. All meals daily. Bus: 72. Map p 99.*

★ Bamboo Sushi LAURELHURST *SUSHI* The country's first certified sustainable sushi restaurant serves guilt-free seafood that happens to be outstanding, too. *310 SE 28th Ave. (at Pine St.).* ☎ *503/232-52550. www.bamboosushipdx.com. Entrees $9–$14; rolls $4–$8. AE, MC, V. Dinner daily. Bus: 20. Map p 98.*

★★ Beaker & Flask INNER SOUTHEAST *AMERICAN* Great cocktails and creative dishes like smoked trout deviled eggs and grilled mackerel with gold beets—even though there's no sign outside.

720 SE Sandy Blvd. (at 8th Ave.). ☎ *503/235-81850. www.beakerand flask.com. Entrees $14–$22. AE, MC, V. Dinner Mon–Sat. Bus: 6 or 70. Map p 98.*

★★ Beast ALBERTA *FRENCH/ AMERICAN* Local celeb chef Naomi Pomeroy's meat-tastic prix-fixe meals—six-course dinners and a four-course brunch—will send vegetarians screaming, but make carnivores swoon. *5425 NE 30th Ave. (at Killingsworth St.).* ☎ *503/841-69650. www.beastpdx.com. AE, MC, V. Dinner $68 Wed–Sat; Sun brunch $35. Bus: 72. Map p 99.*

★ Biwa INNER SOUTHEAST *JAPANESE* Come downstairs into this cozy space for Japanese comfort/bar food like ramen bowls, grilled rice balls, and pickled everything, plus loads of sake choices. *215 SE 9th St. (at Ash St.).* ☎ *503/239-88350. www.biwarestaurant.com. AE, MC, V. Dinner daily. Entrees $6–$13. Bus: 12, 19, 20, or 70. Map p 98.*

BRIX Tavern PEARL *AMERICAN* This fashionable pub offers unpretentious but solid choices like wild-mushroom pizza, mac and cheese, and potpies, plus pool tables and sports on big screens. *1338 NW Hoyt St. (at 14th Ave.).* ☎ *503/943-59950. www.brixtavern.com. Entrees: $9–$23. AE, MC, V. Lunch & dinner Mon–Fri; all meals Sat & Sun. Bus: 17. Map p 97.*

Broder INNER SOUTHEAST *SWEDISH* *Smaklig måltid!* Tuck into Danish pancakes, a Stockholm hot dog, and, of course, Swedish meatballs at this Scandinavian eatery. Their box lunch is a winner. *2508 SE Clinton St. (at 25th Ave.).* ☎ *503/736-33350. www.broderpdx.com.*

Entrees: $7–$14. AE, MC, V. Breakfast & lunch daily; dinner Thurs–Sun. Bus: 10. Map p 98.

★ **kids** **Built to Grill** DOWNTOWN *ITALIAN* Portland's best cheap Italian may very well come from this food cart; try the Tuscan chicken penne, the grilled muffuleta sandwich, and especially the gnocchi. *232 SW Washington Ave. (at 3rd Ave.).* ☎ *503/789-37650. Entrees: $5–$6. No credit cards. Lunch Mon–Fri. Bus: 15 or 51. Map p 97.*

★ **Bunk Sandwiches** INNER SOUTHEAST *SANDWICHES* Nationally known sandwiches? That's Bunk, an unprepossessing spot serving a delectable pork belly *cubano* and roast chicken salad with applewood smoked bacon and avocado. *621 SE Morrison St. (at 6th Ave.).* ☎ *503/477-9515. www.bunksandwiches.com. Entrees $4–$9. MC, V. Breakfast & lunch Mon–Sat. Bus: 6 or 15. Map p 98.*

Cafe Hibiscus ALBERTA *SWISS* Swiss cuisine with a Hawaiian influence (seriously), from fondue to Wiener schnitzel, draws fans to this hidden gem—as does their famous house-made dressing. *4950 NW 14th Ave. (at Alberta St.).* ☎ *503/477-92250. www.martinsswissdressing.com. Entrees $9–$12. AE, MC, V. Lunch Wed–Sun; dinner Wed–Sat. Bus: 72. Map p 99.*

★★★ **Castagna** HAWTHORNE *MODERN EUROPEAN* A prix-fixe dinner here is always a culinary adventure, with fresh ingredients and a mix of textures and flavors. (The cafe next door is less expensive and open for lunch.) *1752 SE Hawthorne Blvd. (at 17th Ave.).* ☎ *503/231-7373. www.castagnarestaurant.com. Prix-fixe dinner $65; chef's tasting menu $95. AE, MC, V. Dinner Wed–Sat. Bus: 14. Map p 98.*

★ **Chameleon** HOLLYWOOD *AMERICAN* This under-the-radar spot earns raves for its intimate atmosphere and covered patio as well as its butternut squash ravioli and coconut cream pie. Most of the veggies come from the chef's own farm. *2000 NE 40th Ave. (at U.S.*

Bunk Sandwiches.

Grant Place). ☎ 503/460-26850. www.chameleonpdx.com. Entrees: $17–$34. AE, MC, V. Dinner Wed–Sat. Bus: 75. Map p 99.

Cheese Bar SOUTHEAST *CHEESE/DELI* Portlander Steve Jones won the 2011 Cheesemonger Invitational, making him the world's top cheese expert, so you know his upscale deli is the place for quality *fromage*. 6031 SE Belmont St. (at 61st Ave.). ☎ 503/222-60150. www.cheese-bar.com. Entrees $6–$7. Tues–Sat lunch & dinner. Bus: 15 or 71. Map p 98.

Chef Naoko Bento Café DOWNTOWN *JAPANESE* This downtown lunch favorite uses organic local ingredients in their noodle dishes, tofu bowls, and bento box lunches (try the wild coho salmon). 1237 SW Jefferson St. (at 12th Ave.). ☎ 503/227-4136. www.chefnaoko.com. Entrees: $7.50–$15. AE, MC, V. Lunch Tues–Sat; dinner Sat. Bus: 6, 43, 45, 55, 58, or 68. Map p 97.

★ **clarklewis** INNER SOUTHEAST *AMERICAN* Sliding garage doors and a fireplace give one of Portland's original farm-to-table restaurants a "cozy industrial" atmosphere, with an open kitchen turning out grilled lamb and black cod. 1001 SE Water Ave. #160 (at Yamhill St.). ☎ 503/235-2294. www.clarklewispdx.com. Entrees $14–$34. AE, MC, V. Lunch

Mon–Fri; dinner Mon–Sat. Bus: 15. Map p 98.

Del Inti ALBERTA *PERUVIAN* Former Andina chef Ignacio del Solar offers picante plates from South America to share, such as seviche and pork-stuffed peppers. Warm up even more at the fire pit in the front patio. 2315 NE Alberta St. ☎ 503/288-8191. www.delinti.com. Entrees $6–$18. AE, MC, V. Dinner Tues–Sun. Bus: 72. Map p 99.

kids Dick's Kitchen BELMONT *AMERICAN* Imagine a healthy version of a diner, with grass-fed beef burgers, natural hot dogs, air-baked "not-fries," and photos of famous, er, Richards on the wall. 3312 SE Belmont St. (at 33rd Ave.). ☎ 503/235-01450. www.dkportland.com. Entrees $7–$12. Lunch & dinner daily. Bus: 15. Map p 98.

★★ **El Gaucho** DOWNTOWN *STEAK* Pricey but worth a splurge, this old-school steakhouse does beef and seafood to perfection, with salads and bananas foster made tableside and live Spanish guitarists. 319 SW Broadway (at Stark St.). ☎ 503/227-87950. www.elgaucho.com. Entrees: $38–$82. AE, MC, V. Dinner daily. MAX: SW 10th & Stark. Map p 97.

★ **Farm Café** INNER SOUTHEAST *AMERICAN* This snug, homey

Brunch on the Bridge

The cornerstone of Portland's week-long Bridge Festival in early August (www.pdxbridgefestival.org) is a one-of-a-kind event that sees the Hawthorne Bridge—all six lanes of it—closed to cars and covered with 28,000 square feet of grassy turf, perfect for a Saturday picnic. Spread your blanket and dig into brunch-y goodies from local vendors (or bring your own); then play a game of croquet or listen to some live music. Proceeds from tickets ($25 adults, $10 kids 6–11) go to charity.

place with creaky floors brings the farm to your table in the form of imaginative dishes like beet carpaccio, herb-crusted tofu, and a standout veggie burger. *10 SE 7th Ave. (at Burnside).* ☎ *503/736-32750. www. thefarmcafe.com/menu. Entrees $11–$22. AE, MC, V. Dinner daily. Bus: 12, 19, or 20. Map p 98.*

★ **50 Plates** PEARL *AMERICAN* Seasonal, upscale takes on American comfort food; hush puppies, roasted chicken, and meatloaf get the Portland treatment. *333 NW 13th Ave. (at Flanders St.).* ☎ *503/ 228-5050. www.50plates.com Entrees $11–$25. AE, MC, V. Lunch daily, dinner Mon–Sat. Streetcar: NW 11th & Everett. Map p 97.*

Fire on the Mountain SOUTHEAST *BBQ* Buffalo wings raised to high art, with sauces ranging from bourbon chipotle and Jamaican jerk to raspberry habanero and the tongue-melting "El Jefe." Great beer selection, too. *1706 E. Burnside St. (at 17th Ave.).* ☎ *503/230-94650. www.portlandwings.com. Entrees $6–$10. MC, V. Lunch & dinner daily. Bus: 20. Map p 98.*

Frank's Noodle House IRVINGTON *KOREAN/CHINESE* Handpulled noodles made daily are the specialty here, but the dumplings and hot-and-sour soup are also worth writing home about. *822 NE Broadway St. (at 8th Ave.).* ☎ *503/ 288-1007. www.franksnoodlehouse. com. Entrees $6–$8. MC, V. Lunch & dinner Mon–Sat. Bus: 9. Map p 99.*

The Frying Scotsman DOWNTOWN *FISH & CHIPS* Worth including for its name alone, this food cart does great British-style fish and chips (halibut, cod, red snapper, or mahi-mahi). *SW Alder St. & 12th Ave.* ☎ *503/706-38450. www.the fryingscotsmanpdx.com. Entrees $7.50–$9. No credit cards. Lunch Mon–Sat. Streetcar: SW 11th & Alder. Bus: 15 or 51. Map p 97.*

The Faux Ho at 50 Plates.

★★★ **Genoa** BELMONT *ITALIAN* The classic plates of Italy—summer bean stew, house-made ravioli— rotate with the seasons at this classy spot in the Sunnyside neighborhood. *2832 SE Belmont St. (at 29th Ave.).* ☎ *503/238-14650. www.genoa restaurant.com. 5-course prix-fixe meal $60. AE, MC, V. Dinner Tues– Sun. Bus: 15. Map p 98.*

kids Grilled Cheese Grill ALBERTA *SANDWICHES* All kinds of gourmet grilled cheese in an old school bus, from the "Kindergartner" to the "Cheesus," a hamburger between grilled-cheese sandwiches instead of a bun. *1027 NE Alberta Ave. (at 11th St.).* ☎ *503/206-89550. www.grilledcheesegrill.com. Entrees $3.50–$8. MC, V. Lunch Tues–Sun; dinner Tues–Sat. Bus: 72. Map p 99.*

Karam Lebanese Cuisine DOWNTOWN *LEBANESE* Friendly service and consistently good Lebanese dishes like couscous, kebobs, and fresh-baked pita bread set this place apart. *316 SW Stark St. (at 3rd Ave.).* ☎ *503/223-08350. www. karamrestaurant.com. Entrees*

Le Pigeon.

$13–$20. AE, MC, V. Lunch & dinner Mon–Sat. Bus: 15 or 51. Map p 97.

★ **Ken's Artisan Pizza** SOUTH-EAST *PIZZA* With an emphasis on the "art," the crisp-crusted pies at this stone-oven pizzeria are worth the wait. Try the prosciutto and *soppressata*. *304 SE 28th Ave. (at Pine St.).* ☎ *503/517-99550. www.kensartisan. com. Entrees $11–$14. AE, MC, V. Dinner daily. Bus: 28. Map p 98.*

Khun Pic's Bahn Thai BELMONT *THAI* It looks like someone's old Victorian house, but it's actually one of Portland's best and most authentic Thai eateries, albeit with leisurely service. *3429 SE Belmont St. (at 34th*

Dining à Le Pigeon.

Ave.). ☎ *503/235-16150. Entrees $8–$12. No credit cards. Dinner Tues–Sat. Bus: 15. Map p 98.*

★ **Lauro** SOUTHEAST *MEDITERRA-NEAN* This contemporary place uses fresh seasonal ingredients in their Greek- and Moroccan-inspired dishes such as braised lamb shoulder and roasted beet salad with pears. *3377 SE Division St. (at 34th Ave.). ☎ 503/239-70050. www. laurokitchen.com. Entrees $17–$22. AE, MC, V. Dinner Wed–Mon. Bus: 4. Map p 98.*

Le Happy NORTHWEST *CREPERIE* Sweet and savory crepes in a charming red-walled nook that seems straight out of a Paris side street (disco ball notwithstanding). *1011 NW 16th Ave. (at Lovejoy St.). ☎ 503/226-12550. www.lehappy. com. Entrees $4–$10. MC, V. Dinner Mon–Sat. Streetcar: NW Lovejoy & 18th. Bus: 77. Map p 97.*

★★★ **Le Pigeon** INNER SOUTH-EAST *FRENCH* An open kitchen and a James Beard Award–winning chef (Gabriel Rucker) make this snug spot a consistent standout, even in Portland. Make a reservation now. *738 E Burnside St. (at 7th Ave.). ☎ 503/546-87950. www.lepigeon.com. Entrees $12–$28. AE, MC, V. Dinner daily. Bus: 12, 19, or 20. Map p 98.*

Leroy's Familiar Vittles SOUTH-EAST *BBQ*   Visit this food cart for melt-in-your-mouth Texas-style BBQ, sweet tea, and collard greens—among the city's best. Don't miss the "burnt" mac and cheese. *SE Division St. & 48th Ave.* ☎ *503/442-74250. Entrees $5–$7. No credit cards. Mon–Sat noon-7pm. Bus: 4. Map p 98.*

Lilikoi NORTH PORTLAND *HAWAI-IAN*   Somewhere between food cart and restaurant, Lilikoi serves tropical comfort food such as their signature pulled-pork sandwich and drunken noodles. *1324 N Killingsworth St. (at Maryland Ave.).* ☎ *503/ 964-84350. www.lilikoiportland. blogspot.com. Entrees $5–$6. No credit cards. Lunch & dinner Tues–Sat. MAX: North Killingsworth. Bus: 72. Map p 98.*

★ **kids Marrakesh** NORTHWEST *MOROCCAN*   Come for the live belly dancing and North African atmosphere; stay for the surprisingly good five-course dinners. *1201 NW 21st Ave. (at 22nd St.).* ☎ *503/ 248-9442. www.marrakeshportland. com. 5-course dinner $18.50. MC, V. Dinner daily. Streetcar: NW Northrup & 22nd. Bus: 77. Map p 97.*

★★★ **Nostrana** SOUTHEAST *ITAL-IAN*   The wood-oven pizzas and

Fresh local fare at Olympic Provisions.

pork dishes get high praise, but it's the little things that make Nostrana special, such as the fresh crushed olive oil and a great happy hour. *1401 SE Morrison St. (at 14th Ave.).* ☎ *503/234-24250. www.nostrana. com. Entrees: $9–24. AE, MC, V. Lunch Mon–Fri; dinner daily. Bus: 15. Map p 98.*

★ **Olympic Provisions** INNER SOUTHEAST *CHARCUTERIE*   The big lighted sign that says "MEAT" sums up this place, with some of the best chorizo, pancetta, and charcuterie plates in town. *107 SE Washington St. (at 2nd Ave.).* ☎ *503/954-36650. www.olympicprovisions.com.*

Olympic Provisions.

banana cream pies and chocolate hazelnut tortes. *701 NW 23rd Ave. (at Irving St.).* ☎ *503/228-73150. www.papahaydn.com Entrees: $18–$24. AE, MC, V. Lunch & dinner daily. Bus: 15. Map p 97.*

★★ **Park Kitchen** PEARL AMERICAN This parkside place has an ever-changing menu of fresh, seasonal delights, both standard-size and small plates (hot and cold) to share. The blind tasting menu is always a hit. *422 NW 8th Ave. (at Glisan St.).* ☎ *503/223-72750. www. parkkitchen.com. Entrees $25–$27; small plates $9–$14. MC, V. Dinner daily. Bus: 17. Map p 97.*

kids **PBJ's** NORTHWEST SANDWICHES Peanut butter and jelly is just for kids? How about one with Challah bread, pumpkin butter, and caramel sauce? That's just the start at this specialist food cart. *919 NW 23rd Ave. (at Lovejoy St.).* ☎ *702/743-0435. www.pbjsgrilled. com. Entrees $4–$6. No credit cards. Lunch Wed–Sun. Streetcar: NW Lovejoy & 22nd. Bus: 15 or 77. Map p 97.*

★ **Ping** CHINATOWN PAN-ASIAN Inspired pan-Asian dishes in a vintage-industrial setting, from baby-octopus skewers to Chinese tea eggs. Come ready to share. *102 NW 4th Ave. (at Couch St.).* ☎ *503/229-74650. www.pingpdx.com. Entrees: $8–$14. MC, V. Lunch & dinner Tues–Sat. MAX: NW 5th & Couch. Bus: 4, 8, 33, 35, or 44. Map p 97.*

Podnah's Pit NORTHEAST BBQ Don't mess with Texas—BBQ, that is, done right at this northeast staple. Pulled pork, ribs, potato salad, it's all Lone Star–worthy. *1625 NE Killingsworth St. (at 17th Ave.).* ☎ *503/281-37050. www.podnahs pit.com. Entrees: $10–$17. MC, V. Breakfast Sat & Sun; lunch & dinner daily. Bus: 8. Map p 99.*

Pok Pok.

Entrees: $7–$14. AE, MC, V. Lunch & dinner Mon–Sat. Bus: 6 or 15. Map p 98.

★★ **Paley's Place** NORTHWEST FRENCH Iron Chef America–winner Vitaly Paley turns out exquisite razor clams and rabbit ravioli in a Victorian home in Nob Hill. If it's nice out, sit on the front porch. *204 NW 21st Ave. (at Northrup St.).* ☎ *503/243-2403. www.paleysplace.net. Entrees: $16–$39. AE, MC, V. Dinner daily. Streetcar: NW Northrup & 22nd. Bus: 17. Map p 97.*

Pambiche NORTHEAST CUBAN You can't miss the colorful building, and the Cuban creole food is just as exciting, from the "Plato Comunista" to the classic pork sandwiches. *2811 NE Glisan St. (at 28th Ave.).* ☎ *503/233-0511. www.pambiche.com. Entrees $10–$20. AE, MC, V. Breakfast Sat & Sun; lunch & dinner daily. Bus: 19. Map p 98.*

★ **Papa Haydn** NORTHWEST AMERICAN Sure, they serve bistro fare here, but what really packs 'em in is the dessert case, groaning with

★★ Pok Pok SOUTHEAST ASIAN
You may not be able to pronounce
the dishes, but Pok Pok's tasty take
on Asian street food makes it a local
favorite. Their Vietnamese fish sauce
wings are a Portland classic. *3226 SE
Division St. (at 32nd Ave.).* ☎ *503/
232-13850.* *www.pokpokpdx.com.
Entrees $9–$12. MC, V. Daily lunch &
dinner. Bus: 4. Map p 98.*

★ ¿Por Que No? SOUTHEAST
MEXICAN "Why not?" indeed—this
colorful *taqueria* is *excelente* in the
atmosphere and food departments
both, especially during sidewalk-din-
ing weather. *4635 SE Hawthorne
Blvd. (at 46th St.).* ☎ *503/954-31350.
www.porquenotacos.com. Tacos
$3–$4; entrees $6–$10. MC, V. Daily
lunch & dinner. Bus: 14. Map p 98.*

★ Prasad PEARL VEGETARIAN
The name means "holy food" in San-
skrit, and the menu is all organic,
gluten-free, and vegan. Choices
include curry bowls, wraps, salads,
and tempeh scrambles. *925 NW
Davis St. (at 9th Ave.).* ☎ *503/224-
39950. www.prasadcuisine.square
space.com. Entrees $6–$9. MC, V. All
meals daily. Streetcar: NW 10th &
Everett. Map p 97.*

★ Produce Row Café INNER
SOUTHEAST AMERICAN Gourmet

Lively vibe at Pok Pok.

pub fare—cheese steaks, meatloaf,
a stellar burger—and an outdoor
patio put this Inner Southeast destination on the map. Try a beer and
whiskey pairing. *204 SE Oak St. (at
2nd Ave.).* ☎ *503/232-83550. www.
producerowcafe.com Entrees
$8–$11. AE, MC, V. Lunch & dinner
daily. Bus: 6. Map p 98.*

Rheinlander NORTHEAST GER-
MAN Sauerbraten, bratwurst,
and *käsespätzle,* with servers in

Produce Row Café.

Pod People

Food carts have become an official Portland "thing," on par with fixed-gear bikes and well-worn rain gear. Maybe it's how they merge the city's idiosyncratic, do-it-yourself vibe with the local passion for good food at a good price. At any rate, there's at least a few hundred on the streets at any given time. They can move, obviously, but they usually park in one spot for a while (hence the listings here; or check www.foodcartsportland.com for updates). Food cart "pods" (clusters) are continually popping up all over town, and a few have started to sink down roots, so to speak:

Downtown:
- SW 5th Avenue and Oak Street (the original Portland pod)
- SW 9th and 10th Avenue between Alder and Washington Streets

North & Northeast:
- N Mississippi Street and Skidmore Avenue (Mississippi Market-place)
- NE 21st Avenue and Alberta Street

Southeast:
- SE 12th Avenue and Hawthorne Boulevard (Cartopia)
- SE 32nd Avenue and Division Street (D Street Noshery)
- SE 43rd Avenue and Belmont Street (Good Food Here)
- SE 50th Avenue and Ivon Street (A La Carts)

lederhosen and accordion music while you eat—Der Rheinlander is a mini-Bavarian village on NE Sandy. *5035 NE Sandy Blvd. (at 50th Ave.).* ☎ *503/288-55050. www.rheinlander. com. Entrees $13–$19. AE, MC, V. Dinner Tues–Sun. Bus: 12. Map p 99.*

★★★ Ringside Steakhouse
SOUTHWEST *STEAKHOUSE* Stumptown's best steak doesn't come cheap, but add an outstanding wine list and onion rings praised by James Beard himself and you'll see why this place has been around for 67 years and counting. *2165 W. Burnside St. (at King Ave.).* ☎ *503/ 223-1513. www.Ringside.com. Entrees $30–$65. AE, MC, V. Dinner daily. Bus: 15, 18, or 20. Map p 97.*

★ Saucebox
DOWNTOWN *PAN-ASIAN* A chic crowd sips creative cocktails and nibbles dim sum and curries as DJs spin in the evenings; earlier, smart shoppers come for the super happy hour deals. *214 SW Broadway (at Pine St.).* ☎ *503/241-33950. www.saucebox.com. Entrees $16–$28. AE, MC, V. Dinner daily. Bus: 1, 12, 19, 20, 54, or 56. Map p 97.*

Screen Door
SOUTHEAST *SOUTHERN* Here you'll find favorites from across the South, including shrimp and grits, beef brisket, and their celebrated buttermilk-battered fried chicken. There's always a line out the door for brunch—for a reason. *2337 East Burnside St. (at 24th Ave.).* ☎ *503/542-08850. www.screen doorrestaurant.com. Entrees $10–$16. MC, V. Dinner daily; brunch Sat & Sun. Bus: 20. Map p 98.*

Shandong Restaurant
NORTHEAST *CHINESE* A bright spot in Portland's subpar Chinese-food

scene, they offer reasonably priced dishes from northern China such as crab curry and cherry pork, plus house-pulled noodles. *3724 NE Broadway St. (at 37th Ave.).* ☎ *503/287-0331. www.shandongportland.com. Entrees $7–$11. MC, V. Lunch & dinner daily. Bus: 77. Map p 99.*

Siam Society ALBERTA *THAI FUSION* Choose from the outdoor patio or the atmospheric interior, and then settle in for pulled pork spring rolls and homemade cardamom ice cream. The bar is lively at night. *2703 NE Alberta St. (at 27th Ave.).* ☎ *503/922-36750. www.siamsociety.com. Entrees $11–$20. AE, MC, V. Dinner daily. Map p 99.*

★★ Tasty n Sons NORTH PORTLAND *AMERICAN* Bacon-wrapped dates with maple syrup are just the beginning at Toro Bravo's sister restaurant, which is just as good. Known for gourmet breakfasts. *3808 N. Williams Ave. (at Failing St.).* ☎ *503/621-14050. www.tastynsons.com. Entrees $7–$19. AE, MC, V. Lunch & dinner daily. Bus: 44. Map p 99.*

Three Doors Down HAWTHORNE *AMERICAN* This neighborhood cafe, hidden down a Hawthorne side street, is a local darling for its happy hour, attentive service, and overall bang for your buck. *1429 SE 37th Ave. (at Hawthorne Blvd.).* ☎ *503/236-6886. www.3doorsdowncafe.com. Entrees $17–$24. AE, MC, V. Dinner Tues–Sun. Bus: 14. Map p 98.*

★ Tin Shed ALBERTA *AMERICAN* Vying for the title of top breakfast in town, this "garden cafe" also does a solid lunch and dinner—but starters like sweet-potato French toast and biscuits with bacon gravy are the real draw. *1438 NE Alberta St. (at 14th Place).* ☎ *503/288-69650. www.tinshedgardencafe.com. Entrees $7–$9. MC, V. All meals daily. Bus: 72. Map p 99.*

★★★ Toro Bravo NORTHEAST *SPANISH* The tapas at "Brave Bull" are so good you might choose to defend them from your friends instead of share. Standouts include duck liver mousse terrine and the salt cod fritters. *120 NE Russell St. (at Rodney Ave.).* ☎ *503/281-44650. www.torobravopdx.com. Entrees $7–$15. AE, MC, V. Dinner daily. Bus: 6. Map p 99.*

★ Urban Farmer DOWNTOWN *STEAKHOUSE* Its dramatic position in the soaring eighth-floor atrium of the Nines Hotel sets off the mostly organic, farm-to-table fare, especially the cuts of beef. *525 SW Morrison St. (at 5th Ave.).* ☎ *503/222-49050. www.urbanfarmerrestaurant.com. Entrees $25–$50. AE, MC, V. All meals daily. MAX: Pioneer Courthouse/SW 6th Ave. Bus: 1, 8, 12, or 94. Map p 97.*

★ Veritable Quandary DOWNTOWN *AMERICAN* With a prime outdoor patio at one end of the Hawthorne Bridge, this 40-year-old institution is known for its *osso buco* and duck confit spring rolls. *1220 SW 1st Ave. (at Jefferson St.).* ☎ *503/227-73450. www.veritablequandary.com. Entrees $21–$29. AE, MC, V. Lunch & dinner daily. Bus: 4, 6, 10, 14, 31, 32, 33, or 99. Map p 97.*

Feel-good food at Urban Farmer.

★ **Vindalho** CLINTON *INDIAN*
"Spice Route Cuisine" leans heavily on Indian recipes but often with a modern twist, such as summer melon *chaat* salad and chutneys with seasonal local ingredients. *2038 SE Clinton St. (at 20th Ave.).* ☎ *503/467-45550. www.vindalho. com. Entrees $15–$19. AE, MC, V. Dinner Tues–Sun. Bus: 10. Map p 98.*

Whiskey Soda Lounge SOUTH-EAST *THAI* Enjoy *aahaan kap klaem,* Thai drinking food, across the street from sister restaurant Pok Pok: dried cuttlefish, drinking vinegars and, yes, those famous fish sauce wings. *3131 SE Division St. (at 31st Ave.).* ☎ *503/232-01050. www. whiskeysodalounge.com. Entrees $5–$12. MC, V. Dinner daily. Bus: 4. Map p 98.*

★ **Wong's King Seafood Restaurant** SOUTHEAST *CHINESE* It's worth the trek way out SE Division Street for Portland's most authentic Chinese food, especially the seafood, chicken feet, and dim sum. *8733 SE Division St. (at 87th Ave.).* ☎ *503/788-88850. www. wongsking.com. Entrees $7–$12. MC, V. Lunch & dinner daily. Bus: 4. Map p 98.*

★★ **Yakuza Lounge** NORTHEAST *JAPANESE* Serving a contemporary version of Japanese bar food, this place offers many small plates to share and an outstanding burger (Kobe beef, of course). *5411 NE 30th Ave. (at Killingsworth St.).* ☎ *503/ 450-0893. www.yakuzalounge.com. Entrees $8–$16. AE, MC, V. Dinner Wed–Sun. Bus: 72. Map p 99.* ●

Portland Specialties

Regional Northwest cooking is distinguished by its pairings of meats and seafood with local fruits and nuts. Salmon is king of Oregon fish and is prepared in seemingly endless ways, but the most traditional method is **alder-planked salmon.** This Native American cooking style entails preparing a salmon as a single filet, splaying it on alder wood, and slow-cooking it over hot coals. Much more readily available today, especially along the Oregon Coast, is traditional **smoked salmon.** After salmon, **Dungeness crab** is the region's top seafood offering. Crab cakes are also ubiquitous on Oregon restaurant menus, and along the coast old-fashioned crab shacks boil up crabs daily. The Northwest's combination of climate and abundant irrigation waters has also made it one of the nation's major **fruit-growing regions,** producing a bounty of pears, blushing Rainier cherries, and berries, including strawberries, raspberries, and blackberries. **Wild mushrooms** are featured on menus of better restaurants throughout the city, so by all means try to have some while you're here.

The Best **Nightlife**

Portland Nightlife

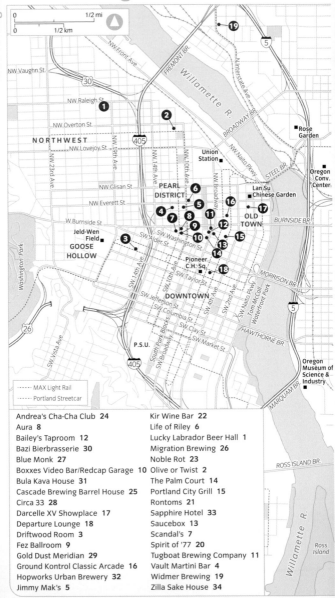

Andrea's Cha-Cha Club **24**
Aura **8**
Bailey's Taproom **12**
Bazi Bierbrasserie **30**
Blue Monk **27**
Boxxes Video Bar/Redcap Garage **10**
Bula Kava House **31**
Cascade Brewing Barrel House **25**
Circa 33 **28**
Darcelle XV Showplace **17**
Departure Lounge **18**
Driftwood Room **3**
Fez Ballroom **27**
Gold Dust Meridian **29**
Ground Kontrol Classic Arcade **16**
Hopworks Urban Brewery **32**
Jimmy Mak's **5**

Kir Wine Bar **22**
Life of Riley **6**
Lucky Labrador Beer Hall **1**
Migration Brewing **26**
Noble Rot **23**
Olive or Twist **2**
The Palm Court **14**
Portland City Grill **15**
Rontoms **21**
Sapphire Hotel **33**
Saucebox **13**
Scandal's **7**
Spirit of '77 **20**
Tugboat Brewing Company **11**
Vault Martini Bar **4**
Widmer Brewing **19**
Zilla Sake House **34**

Previous page: Performance at Jimmy Mak's club.

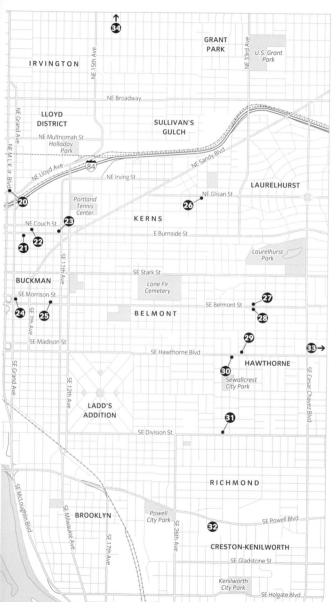

Nightlife Best Bets

Best View
★ Departure Lounge, 525 SW Morrison St. (p 115); and ★ Portland City Grill, 111 SW 5th Ave. #3000 (p 115)

Best Live Jazz
★★★ Jimmy Mak's, 221 NW 10th Ave. (p. 118)

Best Place to Catch the Game
★ Spirit of '77, 500 NE Martin Luther King Jr. Blvd. (p 119)

Best Sake Selection
★★ Zilla Sake House, 1806 NE Alberta St. (p 116)

Best Martini
★ Olive or Twist, 925 NW 11th Ave. (p 119)

Best Dance Floor
Redcap Garage, 1035 SW Stark St. (p 118); and ★★ Andrea's Cha-Cha Club, 832 SE Grand Ave. (p 117)

Best Draft Beer Selection
★★ Bailey's Taproom, 213 SE Broadway St. (p 115)

Best Classy Watering Hole
★★ The Palm Court, 309 SW Broadway St. (p 115)

Best for Romantic Snuggling
★★ Sapphire Hotel, 5008 SE Hawthorne Blvd. (p 115)

Best Drag Show
★ Darcelle XV Showplace, 208 NW 3rd Ave. (p 117)

Best Retro Experience
★★ Ground Kontrol Classic Arcade, 511 NW Couch St. (p 119)

Best Authentic Old-Portland Brewpub
Tugboat Brewing Company, 711 SW Ankeny St. (p 117)

Best Alcohol Alternative
Bula Kava House, 3115 SE Division St. (p 119)

Portland-made pear whiskey.

Portland Nightlife A to Z

Bars & Lounges

★★ **Bailey's Taproom** DOWN-TOWN   A great, wide-windowed location downtown and 20 constantly rotating taps (not to mention dozens of bottles) set this place apart from its competitors. *213 SE Broadway (at Ankeny St.).* ☎ *503/ 295-1004. MAX: SW 6th & Pine St. Map p 112.*

Bazi Bierbrasserie HAWTHORNE Like Belgian beer? Tripel, Abbey, Delirium Tremens—you name it, this place has it (18 on tap at last count), along with Euro-style pub food (Flemish frites!), and sidewalk seating. *1522 SE 32nd Ave. (at Hawthorne Blvd.).* ☎ *503/234-8888. Bus: 14. Map p 113.*

Circa 33 BELMONT   The drinks here focus on the classics—it's named after the year Prohibition was repealed—as well as the cutting edge, with an emphasis on whiskey. Check out the intimate alleyway seating. *3348 SE Belmont St. (at 34th Ave.).* ☎ *503/477-7682. Bus: 15. Map p 113.*

★ **Departure Lounge** DOWN-TOWN   A little slice of L.A. overlooking downtown, this ultra-chic rooftop lounge and Asian-fusion restaurant on top of the Nines hotel has pricey drinks, but the summer views are worth it. *525 SW Morrison St. (at 5th Ave.).* ☎ *503/802-5370. MAX: Pioneer Courthouse/SW 6th Ave. Map p 112.*

Driftwood Room DOWNTOWN The Hotel Deluxe's dim, swank hideaway makes up for its lack of size with tasty drinks fitting the Golden Age of Hollywood theme. (Elizabeth Taylor, anyone?) *729 SW 15th Ave. (at Yamhill St.).* ☎ *503/219-2094. MAX: JELD-WEN Field. Map p 112.*

Gold Dust Meridian HAWTHORNE Practically oozing illicit romance, this candlelit place serves scorpion bowls for sharing under a velvet painting of a nude and boasts the longest happy hour in town (daily 2–8pm). *3267 SE Hawthorne Blvd. (at 32nd Ave.).* ☎ *503/ 239-1143. Bus: 14. Map p 113.*

★★ **The Palm Court** DOWN-TOWN   Two words sum up the Benson Hotel's grand lobby bar: Old School. Stiff bourbon drinks and delish happy hour bites make it a place your grandfather would love, too. Live jazz Tuesday to Saturday evenings. *309 SW Broadway (at Oak St.).* ☎ *503/228-2000. Bus: 1, 12, 16, 19, or 94. Map p 112.*

★ **Portland City Grill** DOWN-TOWN   Arrive early for a window seat to catch sunset from the 30th floor, and you just might stick around for dinner (steaks and seafood) or some late-evening jazz and flirtatiousness. *111 SW 5th Ave. #3000 (at Pine St.).* ☎ *503/450-0030. MAX: SW 5th & Oak St. Map p 112.*

Rontoms SOUTHEAST   Too cool for a sign (look for the helicopter backpack logo), this mod lounge has a superb back patio with a fire pit, planters, and homemade ice cream on the menu. *600 E Burnside St. (at 6th Ave.).* ☎ *503/236-4536. Bus: 12, 19, or 20. Map p 113.*

★★ **Sapphire Hotel** HAWTHORNE No longer the haunt of transient sailors and ladies of the night, this place preserves a maroon, candlelit version of its seamy past, now with food and outstanding cocktails. *5008 SE Hawthorne Blvd. (at 50th Ave.).* ☎ *503/232-6333. Bus: 14. Map p 113.*

Cocktails at Zilla Sake House.

Saucebox DOWNTOWN Nightly DJs transform the bar half of this pan-Asian restaurant into a dark, cacophonous dance club populated by Portland's stylish set. *214 SW Broadway (at Ankeny St.).* ☎ *503/241-3393. MAX: SW 6th & Pine St. Map p 112.*

★★ Zilla Sake House ALBERTA *Kampai!* This sushi spot stocks dozens of kinds of sake—the largest selection west of the Mississippi, supposedly—and they're happy to help you choose the right *junmai ginjo* to go with your Dragon Roll. *1806 NE Alberta St. (at 18th Ave.).* ☎ *503/288-8372. Bus: 72. Map p 113.*

Breweries & Brewpubs

Cascade Brewing Barrel House BELMONT Sour beers aged up to a year in wine, port, or whiskey oak barrels are the specialty of this Southeast brewpub— an acquired taste, for sure, but no one does them better. *939 SE Belmont St. (at 10th Ave.).* ☎ *503/265-8603. Bus: 15. Map p 113.*

★ Hopworks Urban Brewery SOUTHEAST Sustainability is a priority here, starting with the organic beers and food, and extending to the recycled materials used in the

industrial-ski-lodge setting. Cyclists should steer to their **BikeBar** (3947 N. Williams Ave.). *2944 SE Powell Blvd. (at 30th Ave.).* ☎ *503/232-4677. Bus: 9. Map p 113.*

Lucky Labrador Beer Hall NORTHWEST Portland's version of a German *bierhaus* occupies a former trucking warehouse complete with a 5-ton crane in the rafters. Dogs and babies are welcome in this casual spot. *1945 NW Quimby St. (at 20th Ave.).* ☎ *503/517-4352. Streetcar: NW Northrup & 18th. Bus: 77. Map p 112.*

Migration Brewing NORTHEAST The ultra-smooth cream ale on the nitro tap is dangerously good at this

Suds at the Lucky Labrador.

Beer!

With more breweries than any other city on Earth (38 by my count) and half a dozen annual beer-themed events, Portland lays strong claim to being the world's most brew-crazy metropolis. Thank the profusion of local ingredients (especially Willamette Valley hops) and accommodating state laws—but it's mostly due to the sheer enthusiasm and innovation of local brewers, who turn out some of the best lagers, ales, porters, and stouts you'll find anywhere. You could arrange an entire visit just around the city's brewpubs, or take a guided tour of craft breweries aboard the **Brew Bus** ($45, www.brewbus.com) or with **Pubs of Portland** ($30, www.pubsofportlandtours.com). Now if someone could just explain the local obsession with Pabst Blue Ribbon....

casual neighborhood brewery, with picnic tables outside and a dartboard inside. *2828 NE Glisan St. (at 29th Ave.).* ☎ *503/206-5221. Bus: 17. Map p 113.*

Tugboat Brewing Company

DOWNTOWN   The oldest microbrewery downtown fits only 50 people and specializes in unfiltered British-style strong ales. Board games and live jazz in the evenings. *711 SW Ankeny St. (at Broadway).* ☎ *503/226-2508. MAX: SW 6th & Pine St. Map p 112.*

Widmer Brewing NORTH PORT-

LAND   The city's largest craft brewer runs this pub in the semi-industrial zone near the river in North Portland. German food fills the menu, and free brewery tours run on Friday (3pm) and Saturday (11am and 12:30pm). *955 N. Russell St. (at Mississippi Ave.).* ☎ *503/281-2437. MAX: Albina/Mississippi. Map p 112.*

Cabaret

★ Darcelle XV Showplace

DOWNTOWN   This campy cross-dressing cabaret has been going since 1967. Get ready for big numbers, insult comedy, and bachelorette partiers. Shows Wednesday to Saturday. *208 NW 3rd Ave. (at Davis St.).* ☎ *503/222-5338. www.darcellexv.com. Cover $15. Bus: 4, 8, 9, 16, 35, 44, or 77. Map p 112.*

Dance Clubs

★★ Andrea's Cha-Cha Club

INNER SOUTHEAST   Get your salsa, merengue, or cha-cha fix in the basement of the Grand Café, with salsa lessons Wednesday to Saturday at 9pm ($15 including one drink). *832 SE Grand Ave. (at Morrison St.).*

A drag show at Darcelle's.

Jazz at Jimmy Mak's club.

☎ 503/230-1166. Cover $5. Bus: 6. Map p 113.

Aura DOWNTOWN   DJs spin hip-hop, electronica, and party rock on three floors of this downtown lounge across the street from Powell's City of Books. Popular with the college crowd. *1022 W. Burnside St. (at 11th Ave.).* ☎ *503/597-2872. Cover $5–$10. Bus: 20. Map p 112.*

Fez Ballroom DOWNTOWN   This more alternative dance club is known for its "Decadent '80s" nights on Fridays, but it also hosts live music, record release parties, goth/industrial nights, and more. *316 SW 11th Ave. (at Burnside).* ☎ *503/221-7262. Cover $5–$10. Bus: 20. Map p 112.*

Gay & Lesbian Bars & Clubs
Boxxes Video Bar/Redcap Garage DOWNTOWN   Anchoring the "Pink Triangle" gay-bar scene on SW Stark Street, Boxxes is a modern video-lit lounge with a dance floor, while its attached neighbor boasts two bars and a sunken dance floor. *1035 SW Stark St. (at 11th Ave.).*

☎ *503/226-4171. www.redcap garage.com. Cover $5. Bus: 20. Map p 112.*

Scandal's DOWNTOWN   This gay bar/restaurant has been going for a quarter century and has a DJ booth, pool table, dartboard, and great people-watching from the windows. Live locals bands on Thursday. *1125 SW Stark St. (at 11th Ave.).* ☎ *503/227-5887. www.scandalspdx.com. No cover. Bus: 20. Map p 112.*

Live Jazz & Blues
Blue Monk BELMONT   You'll find pool tables and live jazz, blues, and rock Tuesday to Saturday evenings in the basement of this cafe-restaurant on the Belmont strip, plus a full menu available from upstairs. *3341 SE Belmont St. (at 33rd Ave.).* ☎ *503/595-0575. www.theblue monk.com. Cover $5–$10. Bus: 15. Map p 113.*

★★★ **Jimmy Mak's** PEARL   Portland's top live jazz club is one of the best in the country, hosting national acts and the outstanding house band led by drummer Mel Brown in an intimate setting. Come for dinner or just the music. *221 NW 10th Ave. (at Everett St.).* ☎ *503/295-6542. www.jimmymaks.com. Cover free to $20. Streetcar: NW 10th & Everett. Map p 112.*

Martini Bars

★ **Olive or Twist** NORTHWEST More than just a clever name, this friendly Northwest martini bar serves up classic cocktails, single-malt scotches, and a seemingly endless variety of martinis (try the orange blossom). *925 NW 11th Ave. (at Lovejoy St.).* ☎ *503/546-2900. Streetcar: NW Lovejoy & 13th. Map p 112.*

★ **Vault Martini Bar** PEARL House-made lavender-infused vodka and Marvin Gaye on the stereo are just the tip of the iceberg at this fashionable Pearl watering hole. It's small and can get crowded on weekends with prowling singles. *226 NW 12th Ave. (at Everett St.).* ☎ *503/ 224-4909. Streetcar: NW 11th & Everett. Map p 112.*

Other

Bula Kava House SOUTHEAST Portland's first kava house serves the mildly narcotic South Pacific beverage in coconut shells. Kava is definitely an acquired taste, but it's quite relaxing (and legal and non-addictive), an alternative social lubricant. *3115 SE Division St. (at 32nd Ave.).* ☎ *503/477-7823. Bus: 4. Map p 113.*

★★ **Ground Kontrol Classic Arcade** CHINATOWN Tired of the same old bar scene? Come here for two floors of classic arcade games and pinball machines, along with a full bar, and DJs in the evenings. *511 NW Couch St. (at 6th Ave.).* ☎ *503/ 796-9364. Free admission. MAX: NW 5th & Couch St. Map p 112.*

Sports Bars

Life of Riley PEARL Come cheer the Trail Blazers, Red Sox, or whoever else is playing (well, maybe not the Yankees) at this hard-drinking tavern, a welcome touch of blue collar in the Pearl. *300 NW 10th Ave. (at Everett St.).* ☎ *503/224-1680. Streetcar: NW 10th & Everett. Map p 112.*

★ **Spirit of '77** NORTHEAST Named for the year the Trail Blazers won the championship, this new place has high beam ceilings, a

Old-school fun at Ground Kontrol.

Distillery Row

town needed another alcoholic beverage to excel in, recently a half-dozen or so microdistilleries have sprung up along "Distillery Row" on SE 7th and 9th avenues, south of Belmont Street. Places like **Deco Distilling** (1512 SE 7th Ave., ☎ **503/926-7060**) and **New Deal Distillery** (1311 SE 9th Ave., ☎ **503/234-2513**) craft small batches of everything from classic gins and brandies to coffee rum and pepper-infused vodka. Most offer tours and tastings. You can take a pedicab tour ($60) or get a $20 "passport" (www.distilleryrow tours.com) that covers tasting fees and includes discounts at nearby merchants. More information: www.distilleryrowpdx.com.

16-foot-high projection TV, free basketball hoops, and indoor bike parking. *500 NE Martin Luther King Jr. Blvd. (at Lloyd Blvd.).* ☎ *503/232-9977. Bus: 6. Map p 113.*

Wine Bars

Kir Wine Bar NORTHEAST This tiny place focuses on European and "eclectic" vintages, accompanied by small plates of seasonal goodies. A good place to wait for your table at Le Pigeon or the Farm. *22 NE 7th Ave. (at Couch St.).* ☎ *503/232-3063. Bus: 12, 19, or 20. Map p 113.*

★★ Noble Rot SOUTHEAST On the third floor of the red "Rocket" buildings on East Burnside, this wine bar offers wine flights, great views of the city from a glassed-in patio, and dishes using produce from their rooftop garden. *1111 E. Burnside St. (at 11th Ave.).* ☎ *503/233-1999. Bus: 12, 19, or 20. Map p 113.* ●

The Best **Arts & Entertainment**

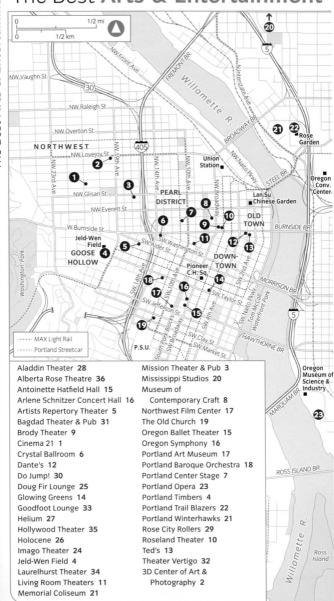

Aladdin Theater **28**
Alberta Rose Theatre **36**
Antoinette Hatfield Hall **15**
Arlene Schnitzer Concert Hall **16**
Artists Repertory Theater **5**
Bagdad Theater & Pub **31**
Brody Theater **9**
Cinema 21 **1**
Crystal Ballroom **6**
Dante's **12**
Do Jump! **30**
Doug Fir Lounge **25**
Glowing Greens **14**
Goodfoot Lounge **33**
Helium **27**
Hollywood Theater **35**
Holocene **26**
Imago Theater **24**
Jeld-Wen Field **4**
Laurelhurst Theater **34**
Living Room Theaters **11**
Memorial Coliseum **21**

Mission Theater & Pub **3**
Mississippi Studios **20**
Museum of
   Contemporary Craft **8**
Northwest Film Center **17**
The Old Church **19**
Oregon Ballet Theater **15**
Oregon Symphony **16**
Portland Art Museum **17**
Portland Baroque Orchestra **18**
Portland Center Stage **7**
Portland Opera **23**
Portland Timbers **4**
Portland Trail Blazers **22**
Portland Winterhawks **21**
Rose City Rollers **29**
Roseland Theater **10**
Ted's **13**
Theater Vertigo **32**
3D Center of Art &
   Photography **2**

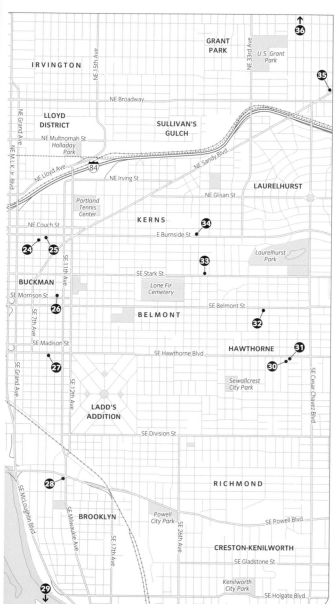

Arts & Entertainment **Best Bets**

Best for a **Beer During a Movie**
★★ Laurelhurst Theater, *2735 E. Burnside St. (p 127)*

Best **Family Entertainment**
★ Do Jump!, *1515 SE 37th Ave. (p 127)*

Best **Popular Music Venue**
★★★ Doug Fir Lounge, *830 E. Burnside St. (p 128)*

Best **Place to Shake Your Booty**
★ Goodfoot Lounge, *2845 SE Stark St. (p 129)*

Best for **Avant-Garde Film Selection**
Northwest Film Center, *1219 SW Park Ave. (p 128)*

Best **Orchestra**
★★ Oregon Symphony, *1037 SW Broadway. (p 125)*

Best for an **Unpredictable Performance**
★ Imago Theater, *17 SE 8th Ave. (p 130)*

Best **for a Belly Laugh**
★★ Helium, *1510 SE 9th Ave. (p 126)*

Best Place **to be Drafted into the Timbers Army**
★ Jeld-Wen Field, *1844 SW Morrison St. (p 126)*

Best Place **for Glow-in-the-Dark Putting**
Glowing Greens, *509 SW Taylor St. (p 128)*

Best **Rough-and-Tumble Entertainment**
★ Rose City Rollers, *7805 SE Oaks Park Way. (p 130)*

Ticket Deals

If you're willing to wait until the day of the show, you can get some good deals on tickets at places like Portland Center Stage, which offers any unsold tickets right before curtain time for $20. At the Keller Auditorium, the Portland Opera offers unsold tickets to students and active military personnel for $10 and seniors for $20. The Portland Center for the Performing Arts has a day-of-show, half-price ticket hot line (☎ **503/432-2960**) for performances at the Arlene Schnitzer Concert Hall, Antoinette Hatfield Hall, and Keller Auditorium.

Previous page: Musicians in the pit at the Oregon Symphony.

Arts & Entertainment A to Z

Museum of Contemporary Craft.

Art Museums

★ **kids** **3D Center of Art & Photography** DOWNTOWN   The history and future of three-dimensional images, from 19th-century stereocards to modern 3-D films. *1928 NW Lovejoy St. (at 19th Ave.).* ☎ *503/227-6667. www.3dcenter.us. Tickets $5 (kids 15 and under free). Bus: 77. Map p 122.*

★ **Museum of Contemporary Craft** PEARL   A low admission fee and a surprisingly deep collection—ceramics, textiles, books as art—make this a pleasant surprise. *724 NW Davis St. (at Park Ave.).* ☎ *503/223-2654. www.museumof contemporarycraft.org. Tickets $2–$3. Bus: 9 or 17. Map p 122.*

★ **Portland Art Museum** DOWNTOWN   This venerable collection (founded in 1892) displays everything from Native American art to Art Deco cars. *1219 SW Park Ave.* ☎ *503/226-2811. www.portlandart museum.org. Tickets $9–12. Streetcar: NW 23rd Ave. Map p 122.*

Classical Music

★★ **Oregon Symphony** DOWNTOWN   Under the baton of music director Carlos Kalmar, the oldest symphony orchestra on the West Coast performs at the Arlene Schnitzer Concert Hall (Sept–May). *1037 SW Broadway (at Main St.).* ☎ *503/228-4294. www.orsymphony. org. Tickets $30–$150. MAX: SW 6th & Madison sts. Bus: 8, 9, 10, 14, 17, or 66. Map p 122.*

Portland Baroque Orchestra DOWNTOWN   This ensemble performs baroque and classical music composed before 1840, often on original instruments, at the First Baptist Church (on Sun at Reed College's Kaul Auditorium). *909 SW 11th Ave. (at Taylor St.).* ☎ *503/222-6000. www.pbo.org. Tickets $25–54. Streetcar: SW 11th & Taylor. Map p 122.*

Comedy Clubs

Brody Theater CHINATOWN   Swing by for a stand-up or improv show or an avant-garde theater production; come back later and take a class. *16 NW Broadway Ave. (at Burnside).* ☎ *503/224-2227. www.brodytheater.com. Tickets free to $12. MAX: SW 6th & Pine St. Bus: 1, 12, 19, 20, 54, or 56. Map p 122.*

★★ **Helium** INNER SOUTHEAST Local and national stand-up acts appear at this slick comedy club. *1510 SE 9th Ave. (at Hawthorne Blvd.).* ☎ *888/643-8669. www.helium comedy.com. Tickets $5–$35, 2-item minimum. Bus: 10 or 14. Map p 123.*

Concert Venues

★ **Alberta Rose Theatre** ALBERTA Catch some live music, an independent film, or a taping of the *Live Wire!* radio show, at this 300-seat restored 1927 movie house. *3000 NE Alberta St. (at 30th Ave.).* ☎ *503/719-6055. www.alberta rosetheatre.com. Tickets free to $20. Bus: 72. Map p 123.*

★★ **Antoinette Hatfield Hall** DOWNTOWN This striking building encloses the classic Newmark and high-tech Dolores Winningstad the-atres, hosting plays, dance, music, films, and more. *1111 SW Broadway (at 11th Ave.).* ☎ *503/248-4335. www.pcpa.com. Ticket prices vary. MAX: SW 6th & Madison St. Bus: 8, 9, 10, 14, 17, or 66. Map p 122.*

Helium Comedy Club.

★★★ **Arlene Schnitzer Concert Hall** DOWNTOWN The crown jewel of the Portland Center for the Performing Arts, the "Schnitz" is the city's most lavish performance space. *1037 SW Broadway (at Main St.).* ☎ *503/248-4335. www.pcpa. com. Ticket prices vary. MAX: SW 6th & Madison St. Bus: 8, 9, 10, 14, 17, or 66. Map p 122.*

★ **Jeld-Wen Field** DOWNTOWN The former PGE Park hosted Elvis and 14,000 screaming fans in 1957; now it's the open-air home of the Portland State University Vikings football team and the Portland Tim-bers MLS team. *1844 SW Morrison St. (at 18th Ave.).* ☎ *503/553-5400. www.portlandtimbers.com. Ticket prices vary. MAX: JELD-WEN Field. Bus: 15, 18, 51, or 63. Map p 122.*

Memorial Coliseum LLOYD DISTRICT The former home of the Trail Blazers now hosts the Portland Winterhawks, big-ticket shows (despite horrendous acoustics), and the kickoff of the Rose Festival Grand Floral Parade. *300 N. Winning Way.* ☎ *503/797-9619. www.rose quarter.com. Ticket prices vary. MAX: Interstate/Rose Quarter. Bus: 35. Map p 122.*

★ **The Old Church** DOWNTOWN Every Wednesday at noon, this 1883

Doug Fir Lounge.

landmark hosts free "Sack Lunch" concerts of classical music by local artists. Other concerts and events through the year. *1422 SW 11th Ave.* ☎ *503/222-2031. www.oldchurch. org. Free admission. Streetcar: SW 11th & Clay. Map p 122.*

Dance

★ kids **Do Jump!** HAWTHORNE With energetic performances that are as much aerial acrobatics as dance, this inventive local company always puts on a show. *1515 SE 37th Ave. (at Hawthorne Blvd.).* ☎ *503/ 231-1232. www.dojump.org. Tickets $5–$15. Bus: 14. Map p 123.*

Oregon Ballet Theater DOWN-TOWN   This company, founded in 1989, performs both classical and modern ballet at the Newmark Theatre within Antoinette Hatfield Hall (see above) and the PCPA's Keller Auditorium (222 SW Clay St.) *1111 SW Broadway (at 11th Ave.).* ☎ *503/222-5538. www.obt.org. Tickets $15–$140. MAX: SW 6th & Madison St. Bus: 8, 9, 10, 14, 17, or 66. Map p 122.*

Film

★★ kids **Bagdad Theater & Pub** HAWTHORNE   This 1927 theater with a pub and two bars shows second-run movies for cheap, along with offbeat performances. *3702 SE Hawthorne Blvd.* ☎ *503/467-7521.*

www.mcmenamins.com. Ticket prices vary. Bus: 14. Map p 123.

★ **Cinema 21** NORTHWEST   One of Portland's most beloved independent movie theaters shows shorts, documentaries, and cult films. *616 NW 21st Ave. (at Irving St.).* ☎ *503/ 223-4515. www.cinema21.com. Tickets $5–$6. Bus: 17. Map p 122.*

Hollywood Theater HOLLYWOOD The city's most ornate classic theater retains its 1926 Byzantine rococo facade and shows independent and foreign films. *4122 NE Sandy Blvd. (at 41st Ave.).* ☎ *503/ 281-4215. www.hollywoodtheatre. org. Tickets $5–$7. Bus: 12. Map p 123.*

★★ **Laurelhurst Theater** LAURELHURST   Pizza, salads, microbrews, and second-run flicks at this restored 1923 theater with the awesome neon sign. *2735 E. Burnside St. (at 28th Ave.).* ☎ *503/232-5511. www.laurelhursttheater.com. Tickets $2–$4. Bus: 20. Map p 123.*

★★ **Living Room Theaters** DOWNTOWN   Combine a European lounge and cafe with an independent theater and you get the chicest eat-in-your-seat movie house in town. *341 SW 10th Ave. (at Stark St.).* ☎ *971/222-2010. http://pdx.living roomtheaters.com. Tickets $9, $5 on Mon & Tues. Bus: 20. Map p 122.*

Mission Theater & Pub NORTH-WEST   This former church and longshoreman's union hall hosts first-run films, live music, talks, and sporting events. Snag a balcony seat. *1624 NW Glisan St. (at 17th Ave.).* ☎ *503/223-4527. www. mcmenamins.com. Tickets $1–$3. Bus: 20. Map p 122.*

Northwest Film Center DOWN-TOWN   The Portland Art Museum's Whitsell Auditorium hosts classic, experimental, animated, foreign, and indie films, plus film festivals and work by local filmmakers. *1219 SW Park Ave. (at Madison St.).* ☎ *503/221-1156, ext. 10. www. nwfilm.org. Tickets $6–$9. Streetcar: Art Museum. Map p 122.*

Minigolf

Glowing Greens DOWNTOWN   And now for something completely different: pirate-themed, glow-in-the-dark miniature golf, in the basement of the downtown Hilton. *509 SW Taylor St. (at 5th Ave.).* ☎ *503/ 222-5554. www.glowinggreens.com. Tickets $8–$9. Bus: 9, 17, or 19. Map p 122.*

Opera

★ **Portland Opera** INNER EAST-SIDE   The Rose City's opera company puts on five productions (Sept–Mar) at Hampton Opera Center and at Keller Auditorium (222 SW Clay St.), including works by Puccini, Mozart, Leonard Bernstein, and Philip Glass. *211 SE Caruthers St.* ☎ *503/241-1407. www.portland opera.org. Tickets $45–$150. Bus: 4. Map p 122.*

Popular Music

★★ **Aladdin Theater** SOUTH-EAST   This 1920s vaudeville house is now a stellar, midsize performance hall for live music from Emmylou Harris to Maceo Parker

Living Room Theaters.

and Ryan Adams. *3017 SE Milwaukie Ave.* ☎ *503/233-1994. www.aladdin-theater.com. Tickets $10–$45. Bus: 9, 17, 19, 66, or 70. Map p 123.*

★ **Crystal Ballroom** DOWN-TOWN   When's the last time you rocked out to Modest Mouse on the dance floor of a 1914 ballroom? Jimi Hendrix, James Brown, and the Grateful Dead all played at this local institution. *1332 W. Burnside St. (at 14th Ave.).* ☎ *503/225-0047. www. danceonair.com. Tickets $5–$30. Bus: 20. Map p 122.*

Dante's OLD TOWN   The Sinferno Cabaret, Karaoke From Hell, live bands, and DJs make this club a tempting destination for a night of dancing and debauchery. *350 W. Burnside St. (at 5th Ave.).* ☎ *503/ 226-6630. www.danteslive.com. Cover free to $20. Bus: 12, 19, or 20. Map p 122.*

★★★ **Doug Fir Lounge** INNER SOUTHEAST   Attached to the Jupiter Hotel, the Doug Fir features alt-rock and great acoustics. *830 E. Burnside St. (at 9th Ave.).* ☎ *503/ 231-9663. www.dougfirlounge.com. Cover $5–$25. Bus: 12, 19, or 20. Map p 123.*

★ **Goodfoot Lounge** LAUREL-HURST   Get up offa that thing and shake it to jazz, funk, soul, Afrobeat, and everything in between. *2845 SE Stark St. (at 29th Ave.).* ☎ *503/239-9292. www.thegoodfoot.com. Cover free to $9. Bus: 15. Map p 123.*

Holocene SOUTHEAST   Booty Basement and Snap '90s Night are just two of the regular events at this dance club. DJs and live music on two stages, and cheap covers. *1001 SE Morrison St. (at 10th Ave.).* ☎ *503/239-7639. www.holocene.org. Cover $3–$8. Bus: 15. Map p 123.*

★★ **Mississippi Studios** NORTH PORTLAND   This venue caters to people who actually want to *listen* to live music in an intimate setting. Good acoustics, and free shows once a month. *3939 N. Mississippi Ave. (at Shaver St.).* ☎ *503/288-3895. www.mississippistudios.com. Cover free to $14. Bus: 4. Map p 122.*

Roseland Theater CHINATOWN   Not the most pleasant live-music venue, but one of the few non-stadium places to see major rock acts. *8 NW 6th Ave. (at Burnside St.).* ☎ *503/224-8499. www.roseland pdx.com. Tickets $10–$40. Bus: 9, 17, 20, 54, or 56. Map p 122.*

★ **Ted's** OLD TOWN   Formerly Berbati's Pan, this small club around the corner from Voodoo Donuts is one of the best to see not-quite-superstars up close and personal. *10 SW 3rd Ave. (at Ankeny St.).* ☎ *503/226-2122. www.berbati.com. Cover $7–$20. MAX: Skidmore Fountain. Bus: 12, 19, or 20. Map p 122.*

Sports

★★★ **Portland Timbers** DOWN-TOWN   The Major League Soccer team fills Jeld-Wen Field with the howls of the "Timbers Army" (Mar–Oct). *1844 SW Morrison St. (at 18th Ave.).* ☎ *503/553-5400. www.portland timbers.com. Tickets $18–$35. MAX: Jeld-Wen Field. Map p 122.*

★ **Portland Trail Blazers** ROSE QUARTER   The Northwest's only NBA team last won the championship in 1977, but they still sell out the 20,000-seat Rose Garden arena (Nov–Apr). *1 Center Court.* ☎ *503/234-9291. www.nba.com/blazers. Tickets average $60. MAX: Rose Quarter. Map p 122.*

Portland Winterhawks ROSE QUARTER   This junior hockey team, part of the Western Hockey League, counts Hall of Famers Cam Neely and Mark Messier among its NHL alumni (Memorial Coliseum, Sept–Mar). *300 N. Winning Way.* ☎ *503/238-6366. www.winterhawks.com. Tickets $14–$51. MAX: Rose Quarter. Map p 122.*

Rose Garden arena.

The Cherry Orchard, *performed at Artists Repertory Theater.*

★ **Rose City Rollers** SELLWOOD
The Breakneck Betties and the Axles of Annihilation are two of the six teams that make up this all-female amateur roller derby league. Catch an exciting (and unscripted) bout at Oaks Park in Sellwood, and occasionally at Memorial Coliseum and the Portland Expo Center (Jan–June). *7805 SE Oaks Park Way.* ☎ *503/784-1444. www.rosecityrollers.com. Tickets $14–$20. Bus: 70. Map p 123.*

Theater

★ **Artists Repertory Theater**
DOWNTOWN   More challenging, avant-garde productions, along with works by established playwrights like Harold Pinter and David Mamet, come courtesy of this first-rate company; their big-red-box theater is an informal, very intimate setting. *1516 SW Alder St. (at 16th Ave.).* ☎ *503/241-1278. www.artistsrep.org. Tickets $25–$50. MAX: Jeld-Wen Field. Bus: 15, 20, or 51. Map p 122.*

★ **Imago Theater** SOUTHEAST
You never know what a night with Imago holds—physical comedy,

animal costumes, mime, dance, acrobatics, music— but it definitely will be interesting. Productions like Frogz, ZooZoo, and Splat are often as entertaining to kids as they are to their parents. *17 SE 8th Ave. (at Burnside St.).* ☎ *503/231-9581. www.imagotheatre.com. Ticket prices vary. Bus: 12, 19, or 20. Map p 123.*

★★ **Portland Center Stage**
DOWNTOWN   The Gerding Theater at the Armory is home of the city's largest professional theater company, performing classic and contemporary works (Sept–June). *128 NW 11th Ave. (at Davis St.).* ☎ *503/445-3700. www.pcs.org. Tickets $24–$65. Bus: 12, 19, or 20. Map p 122.*

★ **Theatre Vertigo** BELMONT
Performing at Theater Theatre's Arena Stage on the Belmont strip, this small but talented company puts on three intriguing ensemble performances every season. *3430 SE Belmont St. (at 34th Ave.).* ☎ *503/306-0870. www.theatrevertigo.org. Tickets $15. Bus: 15. Map p 123.* ●

Downtown Hotels

Previous page: Guestroom at the Ace Hotel.

East Side Hotels

Aloft Portland Airport at Cascade Station **1**
Bluebird Guesthouse **8**
Everett Street Guesthouse **7**
Georgian House B&B **3**
Jupiter Hotel **6**
Lion and the Rose Victorian B&B Inn **4**
McMenamins Kennedy School **2**
Portland's White House B&B **5**

Hotel Best Bets

Best **for Families**
Embassy Suites Downtown $$$
319 SW Pine St. (p 135)

Best **Value (Shared Bathroom)**
Portland International Guesthouse
$ 2185 NW Flanders St. (p 137)

Best **Value (Private Bathroom)**
Everett Street Guesthouse $
2306 NE Everett St. (p 135)

Best **Splurge**
★★ Heathman Hotel $$$ 1001 SW
Broadway (p 136)

Best for **Romance**
★ Lion and the Rose Victorian B&B
Inn $$ 1810 NE 15th Ave. (p 137)

Best **Service**
★★★ Hotel Modera $$ 515 SW
Clay St. (p 136)

Best **Unusual Vibe**
★★★ McMenamins Kennedy
School $$ 5736 NE 33rd Ave. (p 137)

Best **Hotel Restaurant**
★★ The Nines $$$ 525 SW Morri-
son St. (p 137)

Best **for the Hip**
★★ Ace Hotel $$ 1022 SW Stark St.
(p 135)

Best for **Convenience to the
Airport**
★ Aloft Portland Airport at Cas-
cade Station $$ 9920 NE Cascades
Pkwy. (p 135)

Best **for Pampering**
★ Avalon Hotel & Spa $$$
4650 SW Macadam Ave. (p 135)

Best for **Traditional Elegance**
★★★ Benson Hotel $ 309 SW
Broadway (p 135)

Best **for Live Music in the
Same Building**
★ Jupiter Hotel $ 800 E. Burnside
(p 137)

Boho chic at Ace Hotel.

Hotels A to Z

★★ Ace Hotel DOWNTOWN
Stylish from the photo booth in the lobby to the turntables in the rooms, the Ace is a short walk from Powell's City of Books and is surprisingly affordable, befitting a hip young clientele (and their pets). *1022 SW Stark St.* ☎ *503/228-2277. www.ace hotel.com/portland. 79 units. Doubles $95–$250. AE, MC, V. Streetcar: SW 10th & Stark. Map p 132.*

★ Aloft Portland Airport at Cascade Station AIRPORT   Way more chic than your average airport hotel, Aloft boasts large, loft-inspired rooms, free parking, and an overall mod design aesthetic. *9920 NE Cascades Pkwy.* ☎ *503/200-5678. www. aloftportlandairport.com. 136 units. Doubles $99–$189. AE, MC, V. MAX: Cascades Station. Map p 133.*

★ Avalon Hotel & Spa DOWN-TOWN   Head a mile south of downtown to find this contemporary riverside place with great views of the Willamette from room and restaurant and a top-notch day spa to boot. *4650 SW Macadam Ave.* ☎ *503/802-5900. www.avalonhotelandspa.com. 99 units. Doubles $189–$499. AE, MC, V. Bus: 35 or 36. Map p 132.*

★★★ Benson Hotel DOWN-TOWN   Since 1912, the Benson has topped Portland's Old-World-Charm category, now updated with Tempur-Pedic mattresses. Put it this way: Obama stayed here. *309 SW Broadway.* ☎ *888/523-6766 or 503/228-2000. www.bensonhotel.com. 287 units. Doubles $129–$135. AE, MC, V. Bus: 1, 12, 16, 19, or 94. Map p 132.*

★ kids Bluebird Guesthouse SOUTHEAST   Rooms named after famous writers (and Elliott Smith) fill a cozy 1910 Arts and Crafts house within walking distance of plenty on Clinton and Division streets. *3517 SE Division St.* ☎ *866/717-4333 or 503/ 238-4333. www.bluebirdguesthouse. com. 7 units. Doubles $60–$105 w/ breakfast. AE, MC, V. Bus: 4. Map p 133.*

★ Courtyard by Marriott City Center DOWNTOWN   A solid mid-range option in the heart of the city, this Courtyard serves Stumptown coffee and is more contemporary than most. *550 SW Oak St.* ☎ *800/ 606-3717 or 503/505-5000. www. myfavoritecourtyard.com. 256 units. Doubles $169–$199. AE, MC, V. MAX: SW 5th & Oak St. Map p 132.*

kids Embassy Suites Downtown DOWNTOWN   Mostly two-room suites, perfect for families, fill this historic property. Enjoy a great free breakfast and walk to Voodoo Donuts or the Saturday Market. *319 SW Pine St.* ☎ *800/EMBASSY (800/ 362-2779) or 503/279-9000. www. embassyportland.com. 276 units. Doubles $149–$239 w/breakfast. AE, MC, V. MAX: SW 5th & Oak St. Map p 132.*

Everett Street Guesthouse NORTHEAST   There are "no frilly curtains, teddy bears, or potpourri" at this small, stylishly decorated guesthouse, with two rooms and a sleeping cottage with kitchenette. *2306 NE Everett St.* ☎ *503/230-0211. www.everettstreetguesthouse. com. 3 units. Doubles $80–$105 w/ breakfast. No credit cards or children. Bus: 12, 19, or 20. Map p 133.*

Georgian House Bed & Breakfast IRVINGTON   This B&B occupies a historic home befitting its neighborhood; owner Willie is a gracious host who whips up a filling breakfast. *1828 NE Siskiyou St.* ☎ *503/281-2250. www.thegeorgian house.com. 4 units. Doubles $90–$139 w/breakfast. AE, MC, V. Bus: 8. Map p 133.*

Hotel Lucia.

★★ **Heathman Hotel** DOWN-TOWN   Adjacent to "the Schnitz" you'll find a first-rate place with classic service and modern amenities, from in-room French press coffeemakers to a library full of signed first editions. *1001 SW Broadway.* ☎ *503/241-4100. http://portland.heathmanhotel.com. 150 units. Doubles $209–$450. AE, MC, V. Bus: 15 or 31. Map p 132.*

Heron Haus NORTHWEST   Stay in a historic English Tudor mansion within walking distance of Forest Park and Northwest 21st and 23rd ave-nues. *2545 NW Westover Rd.* ☎ *503/ 274-1846. www.heronhaus.com. 6 units. Doubles $160–$215 w/break-fast. AE, MC, V. Bus: 18. Map p 132.*

Holiday Inn Express Hotel & Suites NORTHWEST   Nothing fancy, just a good value at the north end of 23rd Avenue, near where the shopping district veers west on NW Thurman Street. *2333 NW Vaughn St.* ☎ *503/484-1100. www.holiday innexpress.com. 90 units. Doubles $99–$179 w/breakfast. AE, MC, V. Bus: 15, 17, or 77. Map p 132.*

★★ **Hotel Deluxe** DOWNTOWN Step into the Golden Age of Holly-wood at this upscale downtown hotel decorated with black-and-white pho-tos of classic stars. Rooms are snug but well appointed. *729 SW 15th Ave.* ☎ *866/986-8085 or 503/219-2094. www.hoteldeluxeportland.com. 103 units. Doubles $109–$299. AE, MC, V. Bus: 15 or 51. Map p 132.*

★ **Hotel Fifty** DOWNTOWN   A great value for a riverside hotel, this retro-stylish place boasts extra-comfy beds and unbeatable access to events in the waterfront park. *50 SW Morrison St.* ☎ *877/237-6775 or 503/221-0711. www.hotelfifty.com. 140 units. Doubles $119–$339. AE, MC, V. MAX: Yamhill. Map p 132.*

★★ **Hotel Lucia** DOWNTOWN Paintings by Northwest artists and photos by former White House pho-tog David Hume Kennerly set an artsy, contemporary tone and draw a younger professional crowd. *400 SW Broadway.* ☎ *866/986-8086 or 503/ 225-1717. www.hotellucia.com. 128 units. Doubles $129–$269. AE, MC, V. Bus: 4, 15, 31, 32, 33, or 51. Map p 132.*

★★★ **Hotel Modera** DOWNTOWN Outstanding eatery Nel Centro and its outdoor fire pits are just one facet of this luxury boutique hotel that's actually a pretty good deal. *515 SW Clay St.* ☎ *503/484-1084. www.hotelmodera.com. 174 units. Doubles $139–$229. AE, MC, V. Bus: 38, 43, 45, 55, or 58. Map p 132.*

★ **Hotel Monaco** DOWNTOWN Chic, pet-friendly, centrally located—the Monaco, part of the Kimpton chain, is all this, plus it has bikes to rent and a popular happy hour downstairs daily. *506 SW Washington St.* ☎ *888/ 207-2201 or 503/222-0001. www. monaco-portland.com. 221 units. Dou-bles $149–$259. AE, MC, V. Bus: 4, 15, 31, 32, 33, 51, or 99. Map p 132.*

★★ Hotel Vintage Plaza DOWN-TOWN Another Kimpton offering, the historic Vintage Plaza (built in 1894) boasts garden spa suites with private rooftop hot tubs. Among the best lodging in Portland. *422 SW Broadway.* ☎ *800/263-2305 or 503/228-1212. www.vintageplaza. com. 117 units. Doubles $139–$259. AE, MC, V. Bus: 15 or 51. Map p 132.*

★ Inn @ Northrup Station NORTHWEST A colorful retro retreat right on the streetcar line, this all-suite boutique hotel has lots of rooms with balconies and make-your-own waffles for breakfast. *2025 NW Northrup St.* ☎ *800/224-1180 or 503/224-0543. www.northrupstation.com. 70 units. Doubles $139–$219 w/breakfast. AE, MC, V. Streetcar: NW Northrup & 22nd. Bus: 17 or 77. Map p 132.*

★ Jupiter Hotel SOUTHEAST You'll feel like an indie rock star at this eco-friendly boutique motel with its chalkboard doors and illuminated wall panels—or else catch a real one at the attached Doug Fir Lounge. *800 E. Burnside St.* ☎ *877/800-0004 or 503/230-9200. www.jupiterhotel.com. 80 units. Doubles $124–$159. AE, MC, V. Bus: 12, 19, or 20. Map p 133.*

★ Lion and the Rose Victorian B&B Inn IRVINGTON The 1905 Queen Anne building is stocked with

Hotel Modera.

antiques and claw-foot tubs, but the best part may be what's outside: a beautiful rose garden and the eminently walkable Irvington neighborhood. *1810 NE 15th Ave.* ☎ *800/ 955-1647 or 503/287-9245. www. lionrose.com. 8 units. Doubles $99–$249 w/breakfast. AE, MC, V. Bus: 8. Map p 133.*

★ McMenamins Crystal Hotel DOWNTOWN A true rock-'n'-roll hotel across the street from the century-old Crystal Ballroom, this brand-new place has an underground soaking pool, live music at the cellar bar, and tickets to ballroom shows available specially for guests. *303 SW 12th Ave.* ☎ *503/ 972-2670. www.mcmenamins.com/ crystalhotel. 51 units. Doubles $95–$165. AE, MC, V. Bus: 20. Map p 132.*

★★★ kids McMenamins Kennedy School ALBERTA Sleep in a former schoolroom, complete with blackboard, or just roam the art-paneled halls of this former elementary school, probably the most intriguing lodging in town. Restaurant, movie theater, cigar bar, and soaking pool on-site. *5736 NE 33rd Ave.* ☎ *888/249-3983 or 503/249-3983. www.mcmenamins.com/427-kennedy-school-home. 35 units. Doubles $115–$145. AE, MC, V. Bus: 73. Map p 133.*

★★ The Nines DOWNTOWN From its eighth-floor lobby to its rooftop Departure Lounge, the Nines is swank to the max; rooms have a turquoise-and-white color scheme and superb views of the city. *525 SW Morrison St.* ☎ *877/229-9995 or 503/715-1738. www.thenines.com. 331 units. Doubles $229–$354. AE, MC, V. MAX: Pioneer Courthouse/SW 6th Ave. Map p 132.*

Portland International Guesthouse NORTHWEST Six spotless rooms share three full bathrooms at this friendly guesthouse in a quiet

Hotel Monaco.

residential neighborhood. *2185 NW Flanders St.* ☎ *877/228-0500 or 503/224-0500. www.pdxguesthouse. com. 6 units. Doubles $65–$75. AE, MC, V. Bus: 15 or 17. Map p 132.*

★★ Portland's White House

B&B IRVINGTON   This Greek Revival mansion does actually look a bit like the one in D.C., at least from the outside; inside it's pure class, with stained glass, four-poster beds, and antiques galore. *1914 NE 22nd Ave.* ☎ *800/272-7131 or 503/287-7131.*

www.portlandswhitehouse.com. 8 units. Doubles $125–$225 w/breakfast. AE, MC, V. Bus: 9. Map p 133.

RiverPlace DOWNTOWN   The only truly riverside hotel downtown, this Larkspur property abuts Waterfront Park and features L'Occitane bath products. *1510 SW Harbor Way.* ☎ *800/227-1333 or 503/228-3233. www.riverplacehotel.com. 84 units. Doubles $189–$450. AE, MC, V. Bus: 96. Map p 132.* ●

The McMenamin's Mini-Empire

Local brothers Mike and Brian McMenamin opened Produce Row Café in 1974. Since then, they've expanded to almost 60 historic hotels, brewpubs, movie theaters, and music venues across Oregon and Washington. Each of the properties, from the former Multnomah County poor farm (now the Edgefield resort in Troutdale) to their headquarters in a former funeral home in North Portland, bears the distinctive McMenamin's stamp: lovingly restored historic buildings decorated with whimsical art and paintings. Their many restaurants and pubs are fully stocked with their own line of microbrews—they're one of the Northwest's largest craft distillers—but still casual enough for families. (The food is reliably bland.) In Portland they run numerous theater-pubs such as the Mission and the Bagdad, along with the Kennedy School Hotel and the historic Crystal Ballroom. For more info, see www.mcmenamins.com.

Map legend:
- Camp
- Skibowl
- **4** Summit Ski Area
- **5'** Charlie's Mountain View
- **6** Timberline Lodge
- **7** Timberline Trail
- **8** Mt. Hood Meadows Ski Resort

Portland's snowy sentinel juts from the eastern horizon whenever the skies are clear. At 11,240 feet, the stratovolcano is Oregon's highest point, with year-round skiing on the Palmer Glacier, one of 12, above the classic Timberline Lodge. It's an outdoor playground in any season, but especially in winter, when some spots get 500 inches of snow. The road there, U.S. 26, is a National Scenic Byway that follows the general route of the historic Barlow Road, the last and most difficult stretch of the Oregon Trail. (Make a great weekend loop with the Columbia River gorge by taking Hwy. 35 to Hood River.) **START: Troutdale, I-84 exit 18.**

---

1 ★ **Mirror Lake.** A trail head on Hwy. 26 between mileposts 51 and 52 leads to an easy 1.6-mile trail to a picture-perfect lake with spectacular views of Mt. Hood. Keep going to the top of Tom, Dick, and Harry Mountain for an even better panorama. A Northwest Forest Pass

Previous page: Skiing Mt. Hood.

($5/day per car) is required to park at the trail head.

2 **Government Camp.** First settled in 1900, this tiny mountain resort community (pop. 247) sits at the base of Mt. Hood amid fir and cedar forests. It has a handful of restaurants, hotels, and rental condos, making it a good base in summer or winter.

Snowcapped Mount Hood.

❸ ★ **Mount Hood Skibowl.** The closest ski resort to Portland is the country's largest night ski area, with 600 acres lit up after dark near Government Camp. The Cascade Express lift accesses popular cruising terrain and panoramic views from 7,300 feet. It's as much a summer destination as a winter one, with an adventure park and mountain-bike rentals available outside the December through May ski season. *87000 E. Hwy. 26, Government Camp. ☎ 503/272-3206. www.skibowl.com. Lift tickets $59 adults, $49 children 6–12 & seniors 59 and over.*

❹ **Summit Ski Area.** The Northwest's first ski resort, opened in 1927, has a single lift and two downhill runs near Government Camp. It's a good place to learn, and they also have snow tubing and 10 miles of cross-country ski trails designed by a four-time Olympian. *90255 E. Government Camp Loop, Government Camp. ☎ 503/272-0256. www.summitskiarea.com. Lift tickets $30 adults, $20 children 6–12 & seniors over 59, $5 kids 5 & under.*

What **Charlie's Mountain View** lacks in ambience it makes up for in good food, such as the Mountain Cheese Burger with waffle fries, and the wide-window view of Mt. Hood. Check the conditions beforehand on their live webcam.

88462 E. Government Camp Loop, Government Camp. ☎ 503/272-3333. $.

❻ ★★★ **Timberline Lodge.** Built in the 1930s and dedicated by President Franklin Roosevelt, this mountain lodge is full of classic Cascadian character, from its huge stone fireplace and glass tile mosaics to the extensive carved woodwork everywhere. At 6,060 feet on the shoulder of Mt. Hood, it has an unmatched view of the peak and, on clear days, 100 miles in almost every direction. (In the winter you might recognize it from the film *The Shining*, where it stood in for the snowy exterior of the fictional Overlook Hotel.) The attached ski area, with 41 trails and nine lifts, is the only one in the country with year-round skiing. *Timberline Hwy., Mt. Hood. ☎ 800/547-1406 or 503/272-3410. www.timberlinelodge.com. Rooms $115–325. Lift tickets $30 adults, $20 kids 6–12 & adults over 59, $5 kids under 6.*

❼ ★ **Timberline Trail.** You can take it 40.7 miles all the way around the mountain or just do part on a day hike, but either way this is one of Oregon's most scenic trails, ranging from 3,200 to 7,300 feet in elevation. *Access from Timberline Lodge or Mount Hood Meadows. Snow-free mid-July through early October.*

❽ ★★★ **Mt. Hood Meadows Ski Resort.** The biggest resort on the mountain is also one of the best in the Northwest for serious skiers, with 2,150 acres of wildly varied terrain, nine freestyle parks, and a full ski school. Locals know to head to Heather Canyon and Elk and Yoda Bowls on powder days. *14040 Hwy. 35, 10 miles north of Government Camp. ☎ 503/659-1256. www.ski-hood.com. Lift tickets $69 adults, $39 juniors 7–14 & seniors 64 and over, $9 kids 7 and under.*

bia River Gorge

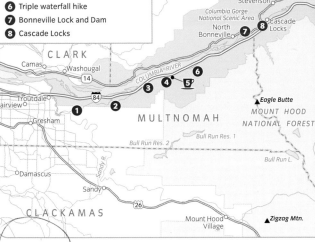

The Northwest's version of the Grand Canyon is 85 miles of basalt cliffs, lofty waterfalls, lush forests, and, oh yes, the barges and whitecaps of the fourth-largest river in the U.S. Much of this National Scenic Area is still as wild as it was when Lewis and Clark paddled through, a fertile gap in the Cascades whose Oregon side alone is a must-do day trip—or longer—from Portland. Combine it with Mt. Hood (p 140) for an even more impressive excursion. START: **Troutdale, OR.**

---

❶ ★★★ **Historic Columbia River Highway.** The best (although not the fastest) way to experience the grandeur of the Columbia River Gorge is the way they did it in the days of speakeasies and Model Ts. Built from 1916 to 1926, the country's first scenic highway was designed for aesthetics as much as practicality, but it was still considered one of the great engineering feats of its time. The narrow road winds for 70 miles along the southern side of the gorge, with dramatic climbs and descents and S-curves, past one amazing viewpoint, roaring waterfall, and 2,000-foot cliff to the next. Many of the distinctive Florentine viaducts crafted by Italian stonecutters are still in place. Start in Troutdale, 17 miles east of Portland, and leave at least a few hours—better yet a whole day—to reach the Dalles (see below), or just Hood River (see below). If you're in a hurry, there's always I-84 along the river. *www.byways.org/explore/byways/2141.* ☎ *541/308-1700.*

2 ★★ **Crown Point and Vista House.** If the Columbia Gorge had a headquarters, it would be at Crown Point, with its 30-mile views from atop a sheer 733-foot cliff. Here you'll find the unmistakable octagonal Vista House, built in 1918 as an observatory and rest stop. Since then its resume has expanded to include a museum and high-end gift shop, and it recently enjoyed a $3.2-million restoration. *3 miles east of Corbett on Historic Columbia River Hwy., I-84 exit 22.* ☎ *503/695-2240. www.vistahouse.com. Vista House open 9am–6pm daily Apr–Oct; 10am–4pm Sat & Sun Nov–Mar, weather permitting. Free admission.*

3 ★ **Bridal Veil Falls.** Five miles east of Crown Point, Bridal Veil Creek tumbles down Larch Mountain and plunges into space, falling in two gauzy plumes for a total of

120 feet. Two trails leave form the picnic tables and restrooms at the parking lot. The short and easy

Bridal Veil Falls.

heads down to the base, ...ger interpretive trail ... the lip of the falls, with ... or the clumsy and agora-phobic. Both trails are under 1 mile round-trip. *Milepost 28 on Historic Columbia River Scenic Highway, I-84 exit 28. Open daily dawn–dusk. Free admission.* ☎ *800/551-6949.*

④ ★ Multnomah Falls. Oregon's highest cascade, and the second-highest year-round waterfall in the country, plummets a total of 620 feet in two steps at the bottom of Larch Mountain. It's a majestic sight, even though its tourist must-see status can bring big crowds on weekends. The scene is enhanced, or at least not marred, by the graceful curve of the Benson Footbridge, built in 1914 about 100 feet over the lower falls. It's part of a 1.2-mile trail that climbs 600 feet to the top of the upper falls, where an expansive panorama and the much smaller "Little Multnomah" waterfall await. Keep one eye peeled; a 400-ton boulder broke off the cliff face in 1995, sending a 70-foot wave over the

Multnomah Falls.

footbridge where a wedding party was having photos taken. (No one was badly hurt, fortunately.) Direct any questions to the information center inside the Multnomah Falls Lodge (see below). *I-84 exit 31.* ☎ *503/695-2372. Open daily dawn–dusk; information center daily 9am–5pm. Free admission.*

Recharge with a bite at the historic **Multnomah Falls Lodge** at the base of the falls, built in 1925. Look for an outdoor table in the summer, but don't bother asking about overnight accommodations; there aren't any. All meals daily. ☎ *503/695-2376. www.multnomahfallslodge.com. $$.*

⑥ ★★ Triple waterfall hike. With 77 cascades on the Oregon side alone, picking which ones to visit can be tough. A relatively easy 4-mile loop trail hits no fewer than three, including an optional fourth, all without climbing over 800 feet. Start at the Horsetail Falls Trailhead on the Columbia River Highway. After ogling 176-foot **Horsetail Falls,** take Trail #400 up a mossy slope to reach 80-foot **Ponytail Falls,** which have undercut the hillside so much that the trail leads behind them. From here you'll climb a bit farther to cross a bridge over the upper end of narrow Oneonta Gorge, before reaching a side trail (#438) that climbs almost a mile to **Triple Falls,** spilling over 100 feet into a large pool. Come back down to Trail #400 and take a left to descend to the Oneonta Gorge Trailhead. From here you can walk east along the highway half a mile back to your car—or else take the stairs down into cool, deep Oneonta Gorge and wade upstream 1,000 feet to **Oneonta Falls,** well worth the dripping scrambles over fallen logs. *Horsetail Falls Trailhead on the Columbia River Highway, 1.5 miles east of I-84 exit 35.*

Windsurfing on the Columbia at Hood River.

7 ★ Bonneville Lock and Dam. Completed in 1936 for hydropower and river navigation, this massive dam stretches 3,460 feet across the Columbia. Four sections connect both banks and three islands, one of which holds the **Bradford Island Visitors Center,** where you can watch through underwater windows as native salmon migrate upstream from October through December. (Fish ladders were added later.) The California sea lions that congregate at the base of the dam gobble so many fish that wildlife officials sometimes have to relocate them. Next to the dam, the **Bonneville Fish Hatchery** (☎ 541-374-8393) raises Chinook, coho, and steelhead salmon and has display ponds where you can feed rainbow trout and white sturgeon. (Don't miss 10-foot Herman the Sturgeon, who's over 60 years old.) *I-84 exit 40.* ☎ *541/374-8820. www.nwp.usace.army.mil/op/b. Visitor center open daily 9am–5pm; fish hatchery daily 7:30am–dusk. Free admission.*

8 Cascade Locks. A series of rapids kept steamboats from ascending the Columbia past this point until a series of locks were blasted from solid stone in 1896. Forty-two years later, most of them have disappeared beneath the rising waters of Lake Bonneville, behind Bonneville Dam.

The upper locks are still above water, though, and are part of **Cascade Locks Marine Park,** with a visitor center, a small museum on river history, and the Oregon Pony, the first steam engine in the West. It's the home base of the **Columbia Gorge Sternwheeler** (☎ 503/224-3900 or 800/224-3901; www.sternwheeler.com), a three-deck paddle-wheeler that gives tours of the gorge. You can cross to Washington on the **Bridge of the Gods,** named after a natural bridge that once stood here according to Native American legend. It's open to cars and foot traffic, including hikers on the Pacific Crest Trail. *I-84 exit 44.* ☎ *541-374-8619. Visitor center open May–Sept, hours vary; museum open Mon–Fri noon–5pm, Sat & Sun 10am–5pm May–Sept. Free admission.*

9 ★★ Hood River. The "Aspen of windsurfing" owes its worldwide reputation to the regular winds that rush down the gorge, sometimes topping 30 mph in the summer. In fact, Hood River is an all-around adventure-sports hot spot, with kayaking, mountain biking, and hiking galore in the gorge and the nearby slopes of Mt. Hood. At night and on the rare calm day, there are plenty of shops and eateries to explore.

Columbia Gorge Sternwheeler.

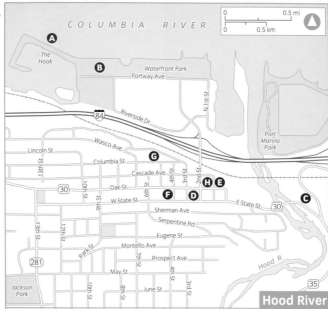

Hood River

You can watch windsurfers and kite-boarders leap whitecaps from **9A The Hook,** a short protected harbor, and the adjacent **9B Waterfront Park,** both on the opposite (river) side of I-84 from town. If you're inspired to give either a try, stop by **9C Windance Sailboards** (108 Hwy. 35 at Hwy. 30; ☎ **541/386-2131**) for rentals and lessons. (Keep in mind that learning here is like learning to drive in Manhattan: difficult, but then you're ready for anything.) To take on one of the many mountain-bike trails on the flanks of Mt. Hood to the south, head to **9D Discover Bicycles** (210 State St.; ☎ **541/386-4820**) for tips

and the largest rental selection in the Northwest. The bulk of the town's restaurants are on or near Oak Street (U.S. 30), including **Celilo Restaurant and Bar** (16 Oak St.; ☎ **541/386-5710**) and **Kaze Sushi** (212 4th St.; ☎ **541/387-0434**). One notable exception is the **Full Sail Tasting Room & Pub** (506 Columbia St.; ☎ **541/386-2247**), one of Oregon's first and most famous craft breweries. If all this makes you want to spend the night, the 100-year-old **9G Hood River Hotel** (102 Oak St.; ☎ **800/386-1859**) is the city's oldest and one of its best.

10 ★★ Hood River Valley Fruit Loop. The river valley between the Columbia and Mt. Hood packs a lot into a small and scenic area: wineries, beehives, lavender farms, and 2.4 million fruit trees, almost a

quarter of Oregon's total. (It's the country's top pear-growing district.) A 35-mile loop drive along Hwy. 281 and Hwy. 35, through the burgs of Dee, Odell, Oak Grove, Pine Grove, and Mount Hood, is an a wonderful

Mount Hood Railroad.

way to spend a day or two meandering from one farm, roadside produce stand, and alpaca ranch to another. (An organized driving route counts 36 stops.) Many of the farms let you pick your own fruit, and festivals from spring through fall celebrate what's in season, from cherries in July to pumpkins in November. *Maps and information available at Hood River visitor center, I-84 exit 64.* ☎ *541/386-2000 or 800/366-3530. www.hoodriverfruitloop.com. Fruit tree blossoms peak in April, fall foliage in Oct.*

⓫ The Dalles. The eastern end of the Columbia River Highway is a historic city at one of the few spots along the river where early traders could easily load boats and canoes. It's full of 19th-century buildings and more recent murals, and the **Fort Dalles Museum** (500 W. 15th St.; ☎ **541/296-4547**), Oregon's oldest, occupies the surgeon's quarters of an 1856 fort. In the mid-1800s, Methodist missionaries preached to Native Americans from **Pulpit Rock,** still standing at 12th and Court streets.

⓬ ★★ Columbia Gorge Discovery Center and Wasco County Historical Museum. Everything you ever wanted to know about the gorge, from the Ice Age and Lewis and Clark through the finer points of how to windsurf, comes together in this exceptional museum. The wide-windowed building itself is a wonder, and its collection spans geology, natural history, and 10,000 years of human habitation, including films, photos, and artifacts. Living history exhibits and a live raptor program round out the experience. Outside, a paved trail connects wetlands, a pond, and viewpoints of the gorge, and continues 4.5 miles to the Dalles. *5000 Discovery Dr.* ☎ *541/296-8600. www.gorge discovery.org. Open daily 9am–5pm. Admission $8 adults, $7 seniors, $4 children 6–16, free for 6 and under.*

Mount Hood Railroad

Experience a bit of time travel aboard a 1906-era railroad through the Hood River Valley. Started as a freight line, it still pulls the occasional freight car but is mostly used for scenic tours to Odell (2 hr. round-trip) and Parkdale (4 hr. round-trip). It's worth it to splurge for the upper dome car, and pack a lunch for the short stopovers. Along the way you'll get views of Mt. Hood and the gorge, and experience one of the few switchback tracks still in use in the country. There are scads of special tours throughout the year, from brunch and Murder Mystery dinner trains to Western Robbery rides and a holiday Polar Express. ☎ *800/872-4661. www.mthoodrr. com. Trains run year-round Tues–Sun, schedule varies, regular excursions $27–$32 adults, $17–$20 children, meal trains and special excursions $45–$82 per person.*

mette Valley

5 mi

km

47

26

8

Forest Grove

Cornelius

8

Hillsboro

SakéOne

McMenamins Grand Lodge

Tualatin R.

Henry Hagg L.

W A S H I N G T O N

Farmington

Gaston

3 South Store Café

Yamhill

5 Penner-Ash Wine Cellars

4 Adelsheim Vineyard

7 Allison Inn & Spa

99W

Newberg

Carlton

8 Carlton Winemakers Studio

47

Dundee

Willamette River

Lafayette

99W

6 Sokol Blosser Winery

M A R I O N

9 Harvest Fresh Grocery & Deli

McMinnville

11 McMinnville

Dayton

18

10 Evergreen Aviation & Space Museum

18

Yamhill R.

1	SakéOne
2	McMenamins Grand Lodge
3	South Store Café
4	Adelsheim Vineyard
5	Penner-Ash Wine Cellars
6	Sokol Blosser Winery
7	Allison Inn & Spa
8	Carlton Winemakers Studio
9	Harvest Fresh Grocery & Deli
10	Evergreen Aviation & Space Museum
11	McMinnville

99W

Amity

The fertile, sheltered valley of the Willamette ("wih-LAM-it") River, the promised land for so many settlers on the Oregon Trail, is now one of the country's top winegrowing regions. It's a kind of anti-Napa, with little of the pretentiousness or crowds, although summer weekends can get very busy. Pinot noir is gospel here, but you'll find other cool-weather vintages as well, including pinot gris, Rieslings, Gewürztraminers, and ever-improving chardonnays. You'll also find roadside produce stands and farms growing everything from tulips to hazelnuts. (**Be warned:** Hwy. 99W can get choked with traffic on weekends, so consider an alternate route.) START: **U.S. 26 west to OR. 47 to Forest Grove.**

❶ ★ SakéOne. Leave it to Oregon to have the only American-owned craft sake brewery in the world. After a tour of the facilities, head to the tasting room to sample their popular blue-bottled Momokawa line, as well as the fruit-infused Moonstone and undiluted "G" brands. *820 Elm St. off Ore. 47.* ☎ *800/550-SAKE (800/550-7253 or 503/357-7056. www.sakeone.com. Tasting room open daily 11am–5pm; tasting flights $3–10 per person.*

❷ McMenamins Grand Lodge. One of the, well, grandest properties in the McMenamins portfolio, this 1922 retirement home is full of all the kaleidoscopic artwork, comfy lounges, and craft beer you'd expect, along with a wine bar, spa, movie theater, soaking pool, and four on-site choices for food and libations. There's even a disc golf course on the expansive lawns that surround the property. The less-expensive guestrooms have shared bathrooms. *3505 Pacific Ave., Forest Grove.* ☎ *877/922-9533 or 503/992-9533. www.mcmenamins.com. Rooms $45–$155 double. AE, MC, V.*

Stop off at **South Store Café** for a pastry, coffee, or a sandwich of house-roasted meat on fresh-baked bread. This century-old clapboard landmark is a convenient tradition both coming and going from wine country. *24485 SW Scholls Ferry Rd., Hillsboro.* ☎ *503/628-1920. $.*

❹ ★ Adelsheim Vineyard. One of Oregon's most popular producers of pinot noirs, Adelsheim has a big tasting room and a patio overlooking the vineyard, perfect for a picnic. Tastings aren't cheap, but you can sample vintages that aren't on the market—including some outstanding single-vineyard wines—and the fee goes toward purchases. *16800 NE Calkins Lane, Newberg.* ☎ *503/538-3652. www.adelsheim.com. Tasting room open daily 11am–4pm. Fee $20. Tour by appointment only.*

❺ ★★ Penner-Ash Wine Cellars. It's a bit tricky to find, but winemaker Lynn Penner-Ash's winery offers outstanding vintages and

Pinot noir grapes, Sokol Blosser.

The Best Side Trips

Carlton Winemakers Studio.

wonderful views from a hilltop between Yamhill and Newberg. Their pinot noirs and syrahs are deservedly famous, but they also make viogniers, rubeos, rieslings, and rosés. *15771 NE Ribbon Ridge Rd., Newberg.* ☎ *503/554-5545. www. pennerash.com. Tasting room open Wed–Sun 11am–5pm. Fees $5–$15. Tour by appointment only.*

6 ★★ **Sokol Blosser Winery.** Whites are the favorites at this popular Dundee winery, the first to receive LEED certification for sustainable practices in the country. Tour the vineyards in their custom biodiesel ATV to see their organic farming techniques and 24kW solar array in action. *5000 Sokol Blosser Lane, Dundee.* ☎ *800/582-6668 or 503/864-2282. www.sokolblosser. com. Tasting room open daily 10am–4pm. Fee $5–$15. Tours by appointment only.*

7 ★★ **Allison Inn & Spa.** This beloved high-end getaway from Portland also makes an excellent wine-tour home base. The rooms are huge, with HDTVs and (in some) hot tubs, and the lush grounds are perfect for strolling and sipping your latest purchase. Relax in the spa and enjoy wine-country cuisine at its finest at the Jory restaurant. What

really earns raves, though, is the attentive but unobtrusive service. *2525 Allison Lane, Newberg.* ☎ *503/554-2525. www.theallison.com. Rooms $305–$355.*

8 ★★ **Carlton Winemakers Studio.** Eleven vintners have banded together under one roof in Carlton, offering tastings of up to 40 different wines. If you're pressed for time or just like to sample a wide range, it's a good choice to visit. The modern building was the first in the country to be certified by the U.S. Green Building Council. *801 N. Scott St., Carlton.* ☎ *503/852-6100. www.winemakersstudio.com. Tasting room open daily 11am–5pm. Fee $5–$20.*

Stock up for your winery picnic lunch at **Harvest Fresh Grocery & Deli,** a natural food store, offering local produce, fresh-squeezed juices and smoothies, sandwiches, and salads. *251 NE 3rd St., McMinnville.* ☎ *503/472-5740. $.*

10 ★★★ **Evergreen Aviation & Space Museum.** In between bites of brie and sips of syrah, how about a side trip to see the largest

Guided Wine Tours

If you can't tell a pinot noir from a petite syrah—or if you just don't want to have to pick a designated driver—try an in-depth guided tour of Willamette wine country. **Grape Escape** (☎ 503/283-3380; www.grapeescapetours.com) runs outings with highly trained guides that include pick-up and drop-off, food and tasting at three wineries in a day ($250 per person for two people; less for larger groups). Half-day tours are $225 per person. **Oregon Wine Tours** (☎ 503/681-WINE; www.orwinetours.com) do the same, with themed excursions such as small producers and "ABP" ("Anything But Pinot"). Their all-day tours start at $160 per person.

plane ever built? Howard Hughes's "Spruce Goose," a wooden flying boat with a 320-foot wingspan, flew exactly once, for 1 minute, before ending up at this hangarlike museum alongside fighter jets, stunt planes, a Mercury space capsule, and much more. There's also an IMAX theater and a new waterpark next door, with 10 waterslides—including four that start from inside a real 747 plopped on the roof—and a wave pool. *500*

Rockets at Evergreen Aviation.

NE Capt. Michael King Smith Way, McMinnville. ☎ 503/434-4185. www.evergreenmuseum.org. Museum admission $20–$27 adults, $19–$26 seniors 64 and over, $18–$25 children 5–16, free 4 and under. Waterpark admission $30 if over 42 inches tall, $25 if under 42 inches. Museum open daily 9am–5pm; waterpark daily 10am–8pm.

⓫ **McMinnville.** Amble down 3rd Street, "Oregon's Favorite Main Street," to find local shops, boutiques, wine-tasting rooms, and top-notch restaurants. *Bon Appétit* magazine dubbed McMinnville one of the country's best small towns for food lovers, and you can see why at places like **Thistle** (228 NE Evans St.; ☎ 503/472-9623) and **Bistro Maison** (729 NE 3rd St.; ☎ 503/474-1888). Even the breakfast spots are four-star: Try the pork meatloaf at the **Crescent Café** (526 NE 3rd St.; ☎ 503/435-2655). The rooftop bar and deck at the **McMenamins Hotel Oregon** (310 NE Evans St.; ☎ 888/472-8427 or 503/472-8427) is the perfect spot to wrap up a wine tour. (The tater tots are a guilty pleasure.)

Oregon Coast

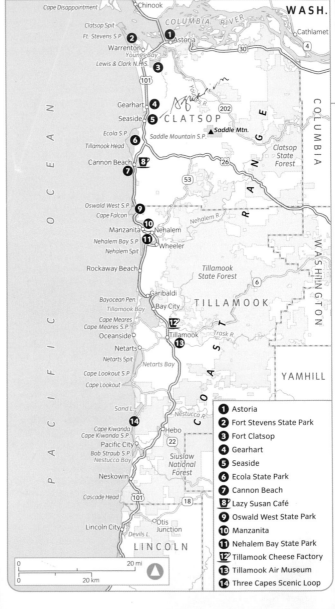

1 Astoria
2 Fort Stevens State Park
3 Fort Clatsop
4 Gearhart
5 Seaside
6 Ecola State Park
7 Cannon Beach
8 Lazy Susan Café
9 Oswald West State Park
10 Manzanita
11 Nehalem Bay State Park
12 Tillamook Cheese Factory
13 Tillamook Air Museum
14 Three Capes Scenic Loop

The northern part of Oregon's coastline gets the most visitors, and it's easy to see why: The thickly forested Coast Range mountains meet the crashing waves of the Pacific in towering headlands and wide, flat beaches, with the occasional rock monolith offshore for punctuation. Sure, it's too cold to swim without a wet suit, but summers are uncrowded by California or East Coast standards, and winter brings its own stormy beauty—plus migrating gray whales. And thanks to a forward-thinking 1967 law, all of Oregon's breathtaking coastline is forever public. START: **U.S. 30 West from Portland.**

Astoria Bridge.

❶ ★★★ **Astoria.** The oldest American settlement west of the Mississippi was founded as Fort Astoria in 1811 by fur trappers working for John Jacob Astor, America's first multimillionaire. Today, restored Victorian homes pepper the hillsides, and restaurants, art galleries, and shops are revitalizing the dilapidated downtown. Spend an afternoon strolling the riverwalk, watching cruise ships and barges pass, and sea lions lounge on piers. While you're there, grab a vegetarian crepe or a plate of local seafood at the charming **Columbian Café** (1114 Marine Dr.; ☎ **503/325-2233**). For more of a workout, climb the staircase inside the 125-foot-high

Astoria Column atop Coxcomb Hill for a panoramic view. Don't miss the outstanding **Columbia River Maritime Museum** (1792 Marine Dr.; ☎ **503/325-2323**; www.crmm.org), with exhibits on the history of the country's second-largest river and the wreck-strewn "Graveyard of the Pacific" at its mouth. If you're inspired to stay, the **Cannery Pier Hotel** (10 Basin St.; ☎ **888/325-4996** or 503/325-4996; www.cannerypierhotel.com) is a modern luxury hotel built on an old cannery pier stretching 600 feet out in the river. *100 miles from Portland via I-5 and U.S. 30 W. www.astoria oregon.com.*

② ★★ Fort Stevens State Park. This 4,200-acre park in Oregon's far northwestern corner is guarded by a fort built during the Civil War to protect the mouth of the Columbia River. It was the only mainland military installation on the continental U.S. to be fired on by the Japanese during WWII—17 shells in June 1942, to be exact. Now it consists of a military museum surrounded by huge concrete bunkers and paths for hiking and bicycling. There's also a lake for swimming and a large campground with yurts and cabins. Head to the park's Pacific beach to find the rusted wreck of the *Peter Iredale*, a four-masted steel sailboat that ran ashore on October 25, 1906. Living history events happen from April to September, including a Civil War reenactment over Labor Day weekend, and you can tour the fort in a surplus military truck in the summer. *8 miles from Astoria via U.S. 101 & Ridge Rd.* ☎ *503/861-1671 or 800/551-6949. www.oregonstate parks.org/park_179.php. Museum open 10am–6pm in summer and fall; 10am–4pm in winter and spring. Truck tours $4 adults, $2 kids 3–12. Admission $5 per car. Campsites $6–$27; yurts $41; cabins $62–$85.*

③ ★ Fort Clatsop. After slogging across half of North America, Lewis and Clark spent the cold, rainy, generally unpleasant winter of 1805–06 holed up in a log stockade they built near present-day Astoria. Named after the friendly local Clatsop Indians, the reconstructed fort is part of the Lewis and Clark National and State Historical Parks group. In the summer, costumed interpreters demonstrate frontier-era skills like making candles and shooting a flintlock rifle. From here the 6.5-mile **Fort to Sea Trail** leads through forest, dunes, and fields to **Sunset Beach State Recreation Area.** *Off U.S. 101, 5 miles southwest of Astoria.* ☎ *503/861-2471. www.nps.gov/lewi. Admission $3 adults, free for children 16 and under. Labor Day to mid-June daily 9am–5pm; mid-June to Labor Day daily 9am–6pm.*

④ ★ Gearhart. If your goal is to get away from it all, even by Oregon Coast standards, then this tiny beach town is for you. Beyond a scant handful of tourist-oriented businesses, Gearhart is just private homes—expensive ones—and a nearly deserted 4-mile stretch of beach. At the **Gearhart Ocean Inn** (67 N. Cottage Ave.; ☎ **503/738-7373;** www.gearhartoceaninn.com), you can steam your own clams in the kitchenettes or walk across the street to the cozy **Pacific Way Bakery & Café** (601 Pacific Way;

The town of Cannon Beach.

Haystack Rock at Cannon Beach.

☎ **503/738-0245**) for a croissant or French dip sandwich. Next door is **Pop's Sweet Shop** (567 Pacific Way; ☎ **503/738-8484**), serving dozens of flavors of Tillamook ice cream. Head to the end of Wellington Street at the south end of town to find a short, unmarked trail to the **Necanicum River estuary,** often packed with shore birds stalking the mudflats for dinner. From here the Pacific dunes are just a short walk west.

⑤ Seaside. Oregon's version of the Jersey Shore brings a little tacky fun to the otherwise staid beach towns close to Portland. The city itself is full of historic cottages dating to the turn of the century, but what draws most visitors is the wide white-sand beach and the 2-mile beachfront promenade, lined with souvenir shops, video arcades, minigolf courses, and amusement-park rides. Lifeguards are on duty throughout the summer, making this a popular beach with families, and there are plenty of places to buy kites or rent three- and four-wheeled beach cycles. At the **Seaside Aquarium** (200 N. Promenade; ☎ **503/738-6211**; www.seaside aquarium.com), one of the oldest on the West Coast, you can touch a sea anemone or feed a seal. *80 miles from Portland via U.S. 26. www. seasideor.com.*

⑥ ★★★ Ecola State Park. Lewis and Clark arrived here in 1806, the farthest south they came on the Oregon coast, to buy whale blubber and see a whale skeleton washed up on the beach. You can trace part of their route on a 2.5-mile loop trail through steep forests of Sitka spruce, or take a slightly longer trail 600 feet up to the top of Tillamook Head, which Clark called "the steepest worst & highest mountain I ever ascended." (It's not that bad, and the views of the coastline are more than worth it.) More hiking trails lead to the beach, a primitive hike-in campsite, and picnic areas on high bluffs, perfect for spotting whales in the winter and spring—and surfers year-round. *Just north of Cannon Beach on U.S. 101.* ☎ *800/551-6949 or 503/436-2844. www.oregonstateparks.org/park_ 188.php. Fee $5 per vehicle.*

⑦ ★★ Cannon Beach. Named for a cannon that washed ashore from a shipwreck in 1846, Cannon Beach may be the prototypical Oregon coast town. It's full of homes covered in weathered cedar shingles, art galleries, shops, and good restaurants and hotels, all without losing its village feel. Visitors pack the place in the summer, but it hasn't turned into a northwest Carmel-by-the-Sea quite yet. **Haystack Rock** is a 235-foot-high sea stack (formed by wave erosion) just off the beach, home to sea birds like tufted puffins. It's surrounded by tide pools full of life—just don't get stranded by the rising tide. Follow up an intimate dinner of lobster ravioli at **Newmans at 988** (988 S. Hemlock St.; ☎ **503/436-1151**) with a night at the **Stephanie Inn** (2740 S. Pacific St.; ☎ **800/633-3466** or 503/436-2221; www. stephanie-inn.com), regularly listed among the most romantic in Oregon. The **Inn at Cannon Beach** (3215 S. Hemlock St.; ☎ **800/321-6304;** www.atcannonbeach.com) is off the main drag but near the beach, with fresh cookies at the front desk. *80 miles from Portland via U.S. 26. www.cannonbeach.org.*

Oswald West State Park.

Grab a marionberry scone at **Lazy Susan Café**. This two-story Cannon Beach cottage is one of the best breakfast spots in town. They're also open for lunch and dinner, with salads, sandwiches, and seafood stews. *126 N. Hemlock St. ☎ 503/436-2816. $. No credit cards.*

9 ★★ **Oswald West State Park.** Mountains meet the sea in a show-stopping way at this coastal park. A 15-minute hike to the secluded, crescent-shaped beach keeps out most of the crowds, except for surfers, who love the constant waves. More trails lead to viewpoints from the headlands on either side, and the Oregon Coast Trail goes up and over 1,600-foot **Neahkahnie Mountain.** Translated as "place of the supreme deity" in the native Tillamook language, the mountain is reputed to hide a lost Spanish fortune that has cost more than one treasure-hunter's life. One trail head is just south of the park boundary on U.S. 101. From there, it's 2 steep miles through dense forest to the summit. *10 miles south of Cannon Beach. ☎ 800/551-6949. www.oregonstateparks.org/park_195.php. Fee $5 per vehicle.*

10 ★★★ **Manzanita.** My favorite getaway on the northern Coast is a 600-person village with one main street and not much to do besides eat, sleep, and go to the beach. It's close enough to Cannon Beach and numerous state parks to enjoy those by day, but all you can hear at night are the waves. The **Ocean Inn at Manzanita** (32 Laneda Ave.; ☎ 866/368-7701 or 503/368-7701; www.oceaninnatmanzanita.com) has 10 condo and kitchenette units right on the sand, and the **Coast Cabins** (635 Laneda Ave.; ☎ 800/435-1269 or 503/368-7113; www. coastcabins.com) are five cedar

Camping at Nehalem Bay.

cottages with a Japan-meets-Scandinavia aesthetic. The **Bread & Ocean Bakery** (154 Laneda Ave.; ☎ 503/368-5823) is one of the better lunch and dinner places in town, with great cinnamon rolls and sandwiches. *14½ miles south of Cannon Beach on U.S. 101. www.explore manzanita.com.*

⓫ ★ Nehalem Bay State Park.
This park covers most of the sandy spit separating Nehalem Bay and the mouth of the Nehalem River from the ocean. You'll find a campground, rental yurts, a small airstrip, and paths for horses, bikes, and joggers. You can take a guided

horseback ride in the summer for anywhere from 1 hour to all day. Or go crabbing, fishing, or sailing around the calm waters of the bay, paddle a sea kayak upriver, or head offshore for surfing or windsurfing. Keep an eye peeled for harbor seals at the end of the peninsula, and look for deer, elk, and even coyotes near the campground. ☎ *503/368-5154 or 800/551-6949. www.oregonstate parks.org/park_201.php. Fee $5 per car; campsites $15–$24; yurts $36; horseback rides $70–$150 per person for 1–2 hours, full day $400.*

The Tillamook Cheese Factory.

After a tour of **Tillamook Cheese Factory,** which produces 167,000 pounds of cheese every day, you can sample the goods at the attached store, including cheese curds (aka "squeaky cheese"), ice cream, and fudge. *4175 Hwy. 101 N. ☎ 800/542-7290 or 503/ 815-1300. $.*

⓭ ★ Tillamook Air Museum.
More than 30 restored vintage planes and helicopters have found a home in the world's largest freestanding wooden building, a former WWII Navy blimp hangar that stands over 15 stories high. The collection

Cape Meares Lighthouse, named after British explorer John Meares.

includes a P-38 Lightning, a P51-Mustang, and a Bf-109 Messerschmitt. *6030 Hangar Rd.* ☎ *503/842-1130. www.tillamookair.com. Admission $9 adults, $8 seniors 64 and over, $5 youth 5–17, free for 5 and under. Open daily 9am–5pm.*

⑭ ★★ Three Capes Scenic Loop. Perhaps the prettiest drive on this part of the coast, this 30-mile route takes you from Tillamook to Pacific City, past view after view of the rugged coast. Take 3rd Street out of Tillamook toward the ocean and turn right on Bayocean Road to reach **Cape Meares State Scenic Viewpoint,** home to Oregon's largest Sitka spruce and the **Cape Meares Lighthouse** (☎ 503/842-2244; www.capemeareslighthouse.org). The 200-foot-high headland is the only place in the U.S.

where you can see three National Wildlife Refuges at once: Cape Mears, Oregon Islands, and Three Arch Rocks. Look for peregrine falcons and gray whales in the winter. Keep going to **Cape Lookout State Park** (☎ 503/842-4981 or 800/551-6949; www.oregonstateparks.org/park_186.php), where a 2.5-mile trail winds through dense old-growth rain forest to the tip of the peninsula, a great place to spot gray whales. There's also a campground (sites $15–$24) with yurts ($36) and a $5 entry fee per car. Past Oceanside and Netarts Bay is **Cape Kiwanda State Natural Area** (☎ 800/551-6949; www.oregonstateparks.org/park_180.php), consisting of sea cliffs, a beach, and a giant sand dune popular with hang gliders. Another giant sea stack looms offshore. ●

The
Savvy Traveler

Before You Go

Tourist Offices

The **Travel Portland Visitor Information Center** is in Pioneer Courthouse Square downtown (701 SW 6th Ave.; ☎ **503/275-8355** or 877/678-5263; www.travelportland. com), which is open Monday through Friday 8:30am to 5:30pm, Saturday 10am to 4pm, and Sunday 10am to 2pm from May through October. For destinations outside the city, contact the **Oregon Tourism Commission,** 670 Hawthorne St. SE, Suite 240, Salem, OR 97301 (☎ **800/547-7842;** www.travel oregon.com).

The Best Times to Go

The start of summer—defined locally as July 4, when the clouds finally retreat—is gorgeous in Portland and all of Oregon, for that matter. Sunshine replaces drizzle, lawns go from lush green to dry brown, and temperatures are warm, but usually not uncomfortably so. From June through September, it's highly advisable to book hotel and car reservations ahead of time—as far ahead as possible for weekends, holidays, and events like the Rose Festival. Spring and fall are more of a crapshoot, weather-wise, but you might hit a week or even two of sunshine. Prices fall and reservations open up in these seasons, and they do even more so in the winter, except around the holidays.

Festivals & Special Events

SPRING April brings the **Spring Beer & Wine Fest** (www.spring beerfest.com), filling the Convention Center with craft microbrews, regional wines, spirits, food, crafts,

Previous page: The Columbia River Highway.

and music. This is also the month to catch the **Tulip Festival** at Wooden Shoe Tulip Farm in Woodburn (☎ **503/634-2243** or 800/711-2006; www.woodenshoe.com), whose fields of vibrant blooms will make you feel like you're in Holland for an afternoon instead of just 35 miles south of Portland.

May starts with the **Cinco de Mayo Fiesta** (www.cincodemayo. org), supposedly the country's largest, which celebrates Portland's sister-city status with Guadalajara, Mexico. Food, entertainment, and music are all on the bill in Tom McCall Waterfront Park. Next is the **Portland Indie Wine Festival** (www.indiewinefestival.com), in which 40 small wineries pour limited-production bottles for expert judges and guests. You can buy wines on-site and have them shipped home, local laws permitting. At the end of the month, the **Mother's Day Rhododendron Show** at Crystal Springs Rhododendron Garden, SE 28th Avenue & Woodstock Boulevard (☎ **503/771-8386**) is a riot of blossoming rhododendrons and azaleas.

SUMMER June is the month of extended events, led by the **Portland Rose Festival** (**503/227-2681;** www.rosefestival.org), the city's oldest (started in 1888) and biggest. Three weeks of events include the **Rose Festival Grand Floral Parade,** a starlight parade, the election of the Rose Queen, a waterfront carnival, and dragon boat races on the river. Some of the events are free.

The middle 2 weeks of the month are also the time of **Pedalpalooza** (www.shift2bikes.org/ pedalpalooza), an only-in-Portland festival of all things bike-related.

Hundreds of events are held, most of them free, including one of the largest **World Naked Bike Rides** in, well, the world; we're talking thousands of bicyclists in the buff. The **Portland Pride Festival and Parade** (www.pridenw.org) happens over a weekend in mid-June, with a Pride Parade on Sunday, live entertainment, a drag race (heels, not wheels), and a pet parade.

Over the extended Fourth of July weekend, the **Waterfront Blues Festival** (☎ 503/282-0555; www.waterfrontbluesfest.com) fills Tom McCall Waterfront Park with 5 days of national headliners. Sponsored by Safeway, it benefits the Oregon Food Bank, and it's the largest blues festival west of the Mississippi. The last full weekend in July brings more beer, this time in the form of the 4-day **Oregon Brewers Festival** (☎ 503/778-5917; www.oregonbrewfest.com), one of the largest and oldest craft-beer festivals in the U.S. Waterfront Park is the setting for close to 100 craft brewers from home and abroad, demonstrations, exhibits, food, and live music.

In late July, indie music fans flock to **PDX Pop Now!** (www.pdxpopnow.com), a free, all-ages festival of local music featuring upwards of 50 artists selected by public vote. When the 3-day event is over, you can take home a two-CD compilation.

The Bite of Oregon (www.biteoforegon.com) in mid-August is a fundraiser for Special Olympics Oregon, featuring food and wine samples from local chefs and regional wineries, along with live music, cooking demos, and other entertainment. Mid-August is also time for another distinctively local happening: the **Providence Bridge Pedal** (☎ 503/281-9198; blog.bridgepedal.com), in which 10 of the city's bridges are partly closed for cyclists. Choose from routes ranging from 13 to 36 miles (or a 5-mile walk) and enjoy amazing views that zip by through a car window the other 364 days of the year.

Summer is also the season of local street fairs on the east side of the city, mostly 1-day affairs with food and drink vendors, music, crafts, and the occasional bouncy castle. The list includes the **Mississippi Street Fair** in early July (www.mississippiave.com); the **Division and Clinton Street Fair** in late July (www.divisionclinton.com); the **Alberta Street Fair** in mid-August (www.albertamainst.org/street-fair); the **Hawthorne Street Fair** in late August (www.thinkhawthorne.com/happenings); and the **Belmont Street Fair** in mid-September (www.belmontdistrict.org/whats-happening/street-fair).

FALL In early September, **Musicfest NW** (www.musicfestnw.com) fills the clubs of Portland with local musicians and national acts for 4 days. The **Time-Based Art Festival** (☎ 503/242-1419; www.pica.org/tba) consists of 10 days of modern visual and performance arts sponsored by the Portland Institute for Contemporary Arts.

Mid- to late October is the season of **harvest festivals**—pumpkin patches, hay rides, corn mazes, and so on—at farms around the city. Many of these happen on Sauvie Island, 10 miles northwest of Portland on U.S. 30. In mid-November, the **Northwest Film & Video Festival** (☎ 503/221-1156; www.nwfilm.org/festivals) brings a plethora of short films, documentaries, and features by independent filmmakers from the Pacific Northwest.

WINTER Get in the holiday mood with the **Festival of Lights at the Grotto** (☎ 503/254-7371; www.thegrotto.org). For the entire month of December, this Catholic sanctuary on NE Sandy Boulevard is lit by 500,000 lights, with puppet shows, a petting zoo, choral performances, and plenty of hot chocolate. Speaking of lights, mid-December brings the **Christmas Ships Parade** to the Columbia and Willamette rivers, with upwards of 50 ships decked out in holiday lights after dark. Head to the Oregon Zoo for the **ZooLights Festival** (www.oregonzoo.org), which includes music, kids' activities, and a special holiday train.

The **Portland International Film Festival** (☎ 503/228-7433; www.nwfilm.org) in February brings 100 films from all over the world to theaters around the city. This same month, the Oregon Convention Center becomes one huge bistro during the **Oregon Seafood and Wine Festival** (www.pdxseafoodandwinefestival.com), which happens in the midst of the Dungeness crab season.

The Weather

Ah yes, the weather. If this almost suspiciously appealing city has a catch, it's what goes on outside from about October to May: mostly gray skies and mist or light rain, with infrequent downpours and sunny days. Hotel rates are lower and reservations are easier to score from fall through spring, particularly along the coast. Bring rain gear, obviously, and a jacket or sweater for night. (Strangely, nothing brands you as a tourist like using an umbrella.) Temperatures regularly drop into the 40s in the heart of winter, when the Cascades are being buried in snow.

But, as locals are quick to remind you, the summers are wonderful, even if they don't reliably start, weather-wise, until the 4th of July. Then you can usually count on 3 months of near-constant sunshine with hardly a drop of precipitation for weeks on end. (Portlanders joke how their lawns are brown in the summer and green in the winter.)

Temperatures seldom climb above the low 90s. This is when hotel and car reservations become essential, especially on the weekends and *especially* on the coast.

Spring and fall are more of a gamble, with occasional windows of sunny weather lasting for a few days or even a few weeks. Even then it's a good idea to have an extra layer ready, ideally one that's waterproof.

Useful Websites

- **www.oregonian.com** is the website for the daily *Oregonian* newspaper.

- **www.wweek.com** takes you to the *Willamette Week* weekly newspaper site.

- **www.portlandmercury.com** is the website of the Portland *Mercury,* another popular weekly.

- **www.travelportland.com** is for the Portland Visitor's Association.

- **www.pdxpipeline.com** offers music, art, and entertainment listings.

- **www.pdxkidscalendar.com** is the place to go for children's events and activities.

- **www.opentable.com**; the popular reservation site offers information and reservations about PDX eateries.

Car Rentals

The major car-rental companies all have desks at the airport, which is the most convenient place to pick up a car. Weekly rates for an economy car in summer can run from $200 to $350, with no discounts, so it's a good idea to shop around. Rates drop in the rainy months. Across the street from the baggage-claim area you'll find the following: Alamo, Avis, Budget, Dollar, Enterprise, Hertz, National, and Thrifty.

PORTLAND'S AVERAGE MONTHLY TEMPERATURE & RAINFALL

	JAN	FEB	MAR	APR	MAY	JUNE
Temp. (°F)	40	43	46	50	57	63
Temp. (°C)	4	6	8	10	14	17
Days of Rain	18	16	17	14	12	10

	JULY	AUG	SEPT	OCT	NOV	DEC
Temp. (°F)	68	67	63	54	46	41
Temp. (°C)	20	19	17	12	8	5
Days of Rain	4	5	8	13	18	19

If you're visiting from abroad and plan to rent a car in the U.S., keep in mind that foreign driver's licenses are usually recognized in the U.S., but you may want to consider obtaining an international driver's license.

Getting **There**

By Plane
Portland International Airport (PDX; ☎ 877/739-4636 or 503/460-4234; www.flypdx.com), located 10 miles northeast of downtown along the Columbia River, is an astonishingly pleasant and efficient airport. You can get maps and brochures from the information booth by the baggage-claim area. Some hotels have courtesy shuttle service to and from the airport, especially the ones nearby; be sure to ask when you make a reservation. The carriers flying to PDX include the following:

- **Air Canada Jazz** (☎ 888/247-2262; www.flyjazz.ca)
- **Alaska Airlines** (☎ 800/252-7522; www.alaskaair.com)
- **American Airlines** (☎ 800/433-7300; www.aa.com)
- **Continental** (☎ 800/523-3273; www.continental.com)
- **Delta** (☎ 800/221-1212; www.delta.com)
- **Frontier** (☎ 800/432-1359; www.flyfrontier.com)
- **Hawaiian Air** (☎ 800-367-5320; www.hawaiianair.com)
- **Horizon Air** (☎ 800/547-9308; www.horizonair.com)
- **JetBlue** (☎ 800/538-2583; www.jetblue.com)
- **Seaport Air** (☎ 888-573-2767; www.seaportair.com)
- **Southwest** (☎ 800/435-9792; www.southwest.com)
- **Spirit Air** (☎ 800/772-7117; www.spirit.com)
- **United** (☎ 800/864-8331; www.ual.com)
- **USAirways** (☎ 800/428-4322; www.usairways.com)

To get downtown by car, follow the signs to downtown via I-205 and I-84 west, and then cross the Willamette River using the Morrison Bridge exit. Without traffic, the trip can take 15 minutes. **Taxis** wait outside baggage claim; a ride downtown costs between $35 and $40. **Blue Star** ☎ 503/249-1837; www.bluestarbus.com) runs a shared shuttle bus to the airport for $14 per person each way to and from downtown.

The airport is also at one end of the **MAX light-rail** Red Line. Trains leave daily about every 15 minutes between 5am and midnight, and it takes 35 to 40 minutes to get to Pioneer Courthouse Square in the heart of downtown. You can reach destinations in the Southeast, Northeast, and Northwest parts of the city by getting off at an earlier stop and transferring to a city bus. The adult MAX fare is $2.40. For information on this service, contact **TriMet** (☎ **503/238-7433;** www.trimet.org).

By Car

Portland is 175 miles from Seattle; 285 miles from Vancouver, British Columbia; 640 miles from San Francisco; and 1,015 miles from Los Angeles, all via **I-5,** the interstate backbone of the West Coast. Starting in Portland, **I-84** runs east to Idaho and Utah.

By Train

Amtrak trains stop at the historic **Union Station,** 800 NW 6th Ave. (☎ **800/872-7245** or 503/273-4860; www.amtrak.com), 12 blocks from Pioneer Courthouse Square. *The Coast Starlight* train runs from Seattle to Los Angeles, stopping at Portland, Sacramento, San Francisco, and Santa Barbara. *The Empire Builder* heads east to Chicago via Spokane, St. Paul/Minneapolis, and Milwaukee. The Amtrak *Cascades* (www.amtrakcascades.com) is a sleek, European-style train that makes the run between Portland and Seattle in 3½ hours versus 4½ hours for the regular train. The whole Cascades route extends from Eugene, Oregon, to Vancouver, British Columbia. On either type of train, one-way fares between Seattle and Portland run $39 to $52.

As at the airport, taxis are usually waiting outside, and you might be able to get your hotel to send a van to pick you up. If you're renting a car from a downtown car-rental office, the agency will usually pick you up at the station. The MAX green and yellow lines stop about a block away at NW 6th Avenue, and Hoyt Street Bus routes 7, 9, and 33 stop within a block of the station to the south, toward downtown.

By Bus

The **Greyhound Bus Lines** station is at 550 NW 6th Ave. (☎ **800/231-2222** or 503/243-2361; www.greyhound.com), just across NW Irving Street from Union Station. As with getting into downtown from the train station, there is no charge to ride any public city bus (see below) if you catch it outside the Greyhound terminal, which is within Portland's Fareless Square area. The Union Station/NW 6th & Hoyt Street MAX stop for the green and yellow lines is right outside, as are stops for the city bus routes 7, 9, and 33.

Getting **Around**

One of the best things about Portland's enviable public transport system is that a big chunk in the heart of it is free. The **Free Rail Zone** covers most of downtown and part of Old Town/Chinatown, bordered by I-405, NW Irving Street, and the Willamette River. It also extends across the Steel Bridge to enclose the Rose Quarter (site of the Oregon Convention Center and the Rose Garden arena) and the Lloyd District (home of the Lloyd Center Mall). Inside this zone, the MAX light-rail and Portland Streetcar are both free—all day, every day.

Navigation

Finding an address in Portland can be simple. As in Washington, D.C., almost all addresses here are tagged with a map quadrant: **NE** (northeast), **SW** (southwest), and so forth. The dividing lines are the Willamette River between east and west and Burnside Street between north and south. (Burnside itself is split into "East" and "West" on either side of the river.) That means all of downtown is either NW (northwest) or SW (southwest). It also means you can have the same street name on both sides of the river, just in different quadrants—say, SW Salmon Street and SE Salmon Street. The only exception is North Portland, a big wedge of the city on the east side of the Willamette between I-5 (to the east) and the river (to the west). Addresses here are simply "North" whatever.

Other navigational quirks: Avenues run north to south and streets run east to west; street names in Northwest Portland are alphabetical heading north from Burnside to Wilson; and on the west side, what would be 7th and 8th avenues are instead named Broadway and Park avenues, respectively.

By Light Rail
The **Metropolitan Area Express**
(MAX) is Portland's aboveground light-rail system, connecting downtown with the airport, the eastern suburb of Gresham, the western suburbs of Beaverton and Hillsboro, and North Portland. It's administered, like the buses and streetcars, by **TriMet** (**503/238-7433;** www.trimet.org), with a ticket office behind the waterfall fountain at Pioneer Courthouse Square, open Monday through Friday from 8:30am to 5:30pm. You can also buy tickets at most local Albertsons, Fred Meyers, and Safeway stores. Their website is useful for planning trips.

If you're traveling outside the Free Rail Zone, be sure to buy a **ticket** and stamp it in the time-punch machine on the platform before you board the MAX. There are ticket-vending machines at all MAX stops that tell you how much to pay and give change. (MAX drivers cannot sell tickets.) Fares are the same as on buses and streetcars: $2.10 to $2.40, depending on how far you travel. Seniors 65 years and older pay $1 with valid proof of age; children 7 through 17 pay $1.50. Ticket inspectors randomly check to make sure passengers have stamped tickets. All-day tickets that cost $5 are good for travel to all zones and are valid on buses, streetcars, and the MAX. Transfers to TriMet buses and streetcars are free. MAX cars have hooks for hanging bicycles inside, though they tend to fill up fast.

On certain Sundays from May through Christmas, free **vintage trolleys** run along the MAX green and yellow lines around the Portland Transit Mall (btw. 5th and 6th aves. from Union Station to Portland State University.) Replicas of streetcars that plied the city from 1904 to 1950, they run every 30 minutes from 10:30am to 5:15pm and stop at all MAX stations.

By Streetcar
The **Portland Streetcar** (www.portlandstreetcar.org) runs a 4-mile route from the South Waterfront District (site of the lower Oregon Heath & Science University campus and the Portland Aerial Tram) past Riverplace and Portland State University, through downtown and the Pearl District, and into Northwest Portland at Legacy Good Samaritan Hospital at NW 23rd Avenue, on Lovejoy and Northrup. Fares outside the Free Rail Zone are the same as for buses and the MAX (see above). Cars run about every 13 to 20

minutes daily from 5:30am to 11:30pm on weekdays, 7:15am to 11:30pm on Saturday, and 7:15am to 10:30pm on Sunday.

In 2009, ground was broken on a new 3.3-mile streetcar route across the river, connecting downtown with the Rose Quarter, the Convention Center, the Lloyd District, and OMSI. Scheduled to open in fall 2012, the Loop Project will cross the Broadway Bridge and a new bridge between OHSU and OMSI, adding another 28 stops mostly along Martin Luther King, Jr., and Grand avenues.

By Bus

TriMet buses operate daily over an extensive network, stretching from Forest Grove to Gresham and from North Portland to Oregon City. Just over half the bus lines run about every 15 minutes during the morning and afternoon rush hours on weekdays. Service is less frequent in the early morning, midday, and evening. Fares outside the Free Rail Zone are the same as for the streetcar and the MAX (see above). Every bus has a rack on the front that can hold two bikes. They can be a little tricky to operate the first time; check their website for instructions.

By Car

Oregon drivers tend to be on the civil side; if you honk your horn in anything but a serious situation, you'll find you get funny looks or worse. Speaking of which, expect the same if you try to pump your own gas: Oregon and New Jersey are the only two states where attendants are required to do this for you. It's illegal to text or talk on a cellphone while driving without using a hands-free accessory—and even that's illegal if you're under 18.

You may turn right on a red light after a full stop, and if you are in the far-left lane of a one-way street, you may turn left into the adjacent left lane of a one-way street at a red light after a full stop. Everyone in a moving vehicle is required to wear a seat belt.

Portlanders are generally used to driving with bicyclists on the road, but visiting drivers should be extra wary, especially at night and in the rain, since some suicidal bikers refuse to use lights or wear helmets. As traffic goes, Portland ranks in the top 20% of cities with bad congestion nationwide. I-5, I-84, and I-205 all often back up during rush hour, when bridges and interchanges turn into chokepoints.

Many of the blocks in downtown, the Pearl District, and the Lloyd District have electronic SmartMeter pay stations for **street parking.** These take cash and credit cards and spit out parking receipts that you attach to your curbside window. One benefit is that you can use your remaining time at another parking space. You're generally required to pay from 8am to 7pm Monday through Saturday and 1 to 7pm on Sunday, and the rate is $1 to $1.60 per hour.

The best parking deal in town is the six city-owned **SmartPark garages** (☎ 503/790-9300) downtown with nearly 4,000 public spaces. Four of these are open 24/7. Rates are $1.50 per hour for the first 4 hours and $3–$5 per hour after that. All-day parking is $7–$15 on weekdays and $5 on weekends. You'll find SmartPark garages at 1st Avenue and Jefferson Street, 4th Avenue and Yamhill Street, 10th Avenue and Yamhill Street, 3rd Avenue and Alder Street, O'Bryant Square, Naito Parkway and Davis Street, and Station Place (in the Pearl District near Union Station). Hundreds of downtown merchants validate SmartPark tickets for a short stay if you spend a certain minimum, although this varies.

A car is by far the best way to access points outside the city. There just isn't any other way to get to the more remote natural spectacles or to fully appreciate such regions as the Oregon coast or eastern Oregon.

It takes about 1½ hours to drive from Portland to Cannon Beach on the Oregon coast; from Portland to Mount Hood, about 1 hour, depending on traffic.

Car-sharing in America was born in Portland in 1998, and today **Zipcar** has hundreds of vehicles parked around the metro area. They have an office downtown at 739 SW 10th Ave. and Yamhill Street (☎ **503/328-3539** or 866-494-7227; www.zipcar.com).

The **American Automobile Association** (www.aaaorid.com) has a Portland office at 600 SW Market St. (☎ **503/222-6767** or 800/452-1643), which offers free city maps to members.

By Taxi

Although there are almost always taxis waiting in line at major hotels, you won't find them cruising the streets—you'll have to call ahead for one. **Broadway Cab** (☎ **503/227-1234;** www.broadwaycab.com) charges $2.50 per mile and $1 for each additional passenger, with a $2.50 airport pickup surcharge.

By Bike

Have you gathered by now that Portlanders are somewhat fond of **bicycling?** Being chosen as the country's first platinum-level Bicycle Friendly Community from the League of American Bicyclists in 2009 is just one of the city's many cycling accolades. A progressive citywide bike transportation program includes ubiquitous bike racks and wide, clear bike lanes on most major commuter routes. Riders are required to obey all traffic laws—cops give out real tickets for not coming to a full stop at stop signs, for instance—and you have to give pedestrians right-of-way on sidewalks (obviously). For more information and news about biking in Portland, check out **BikePortland** (www.bikeportland.org) or the nonprofit **Bicycle Transportation Alliance** (☎ 503/226-0676; www.bta4bikes.org).

Cross a bike with a taxi and you get a **pedicab.** You can hail these three-wheeled cycles-for-hire downtown or call ahead for a pickup. Rates vary—most short trips are $10–$20—and drivers work for tips. Try **PDX Pedicabs** (☎ **503/828-9888;** www.pdxpedicab.com) or **Portland Pedicabs** (☎ **503/329-2575;** www.portlandpedals.com). Both offer special guided tours of local brewpubs, distilleries, and the like.

Fast **Facts**

AREA CODE The area code for most of Portland is **503,** although a **971** crops up occasionally. For the rest of Oregon, the area codes are **541** and **458.** On the other side of the Columbia River in Washington, it's **360** from the coast through Vancouver and **509** beyond Cascade Locks.

BABYSITTERS If your hotel doesn't offer babysitting services, call

Northwest Nannies (☎ 503/245-5288; www.nwnanny.com).

BUSINESS HOURS In general, stores are open weekdays 9 or 10am to 5 or 6pm, and Sunday noon to 5pm. Malls can stay open to 9pm Monday to Saturday, and many art galleries and antiques stores are closed on Monday. Banks are open Monday to Friday 9am to 5pm (occasionally Sat

9am–noon). Bars and clubs can stay open until 2am.

DENTIST Contact the **Multnomah Dental Society** (☎ **503/513-5010**; www.multnomahdental.org) for a referral.

DISABLED TRAVELERS Wheelchair users will find most of the city relatively flat, outside of the West Hills and geologic anomalies like Mount Tabor. Most hotels provide wheelchair-accessible rooms, and some of the larger and more expensive hotels also have TDD telephones and other amenities for the hearing- and sight-impaired. Sidewalk ramps are the norm downtown but seem more randomly placed elsewhere. Organizations that offer resources and assistance to travelers with disabilities include **MossRehab** (☎ **215/663-6000**; www.mossresourcenet.org/travel.htm); the **American Foundation for the Blind** (☎ **800/232-5463**; www.afb.org); and the **Society for Accessible Travel & Hospitality** (☎ **212/447-7284**; www.sath.org).

DOCTORS See "Hospitals," below.

DRINKING LAWS The legal minimum drinking age in Oregon is 21. Beer and wine are available in grocery stores and convenience stores, and hard liquor can be purchased in bars, restaurants, and liquor stores. Brewpubs tend to sell only beer and wine, but some also have hard liquor licenses.

ELECTRICITY The U.S. uses 110–120 volts AC (60 cycles). You'll need a 110-volt transformer and a plug adapter with two flat parallel pins to use 220–240 volt appliances. (It's best to bring one from home.)

EMBASSIES & CONSULATES All embassies are in the nation's capital, Washington, D.C. Some consulates are in major U.S. cities, and most nations have a mission to the United Nations in New York City. If your country isn't listed below, call

for directory information in Washington, D.C. (☎ **202/555-1212**) or check www.embassy.org/embassies.

The embassy of **Australia** is at 1601 Massachusetts Ave. NW, Washington, DC 20036 (☎ **202/797-3000**; www.usa.embassy.gov.au). Consulates are in New York, Honolulu, Houston, Los Angeles, and San Francisco.

The embassy of **Canada** is at 501 Pennsylvania Ave. NW, Washington, DC 20001 (☎ **202/682-1740**; www.canadainternational.gc.ca/washington). Other Canadian consulates are in Buffalo (New York), Detroit, Los Angeles, New York, and Seattle.

The embassy of **Ireland** is at 2234 Massachusetts Ave. NW, Washington, DC 20008 (☎ **202/462-3939**; www.embassyofireland.org). Irish consulates are in Boston, Chicago, New York, San Francisco, and other cities. See website for complete listing.

The embassy of **New Zealand** is at 37 Observatory Circle NW, Washington, DC 20008 (☎ **202/328-4800**; www.nzembassy.com). New Zealand consulates are in Los Angeles, Salt Lake City, San Francisco, and Seattle.

The embassy of the **United Kingdom** is at 3100 Massachusetts Ave. NW, Washington, DC 20008 (☎ **202/588-6500**; http://ukinusa.fco.gov.uk). Other British consulates are in Atlanta, Boston, Chicago, Cleveland, Houston, Los Angeles, New York, San Francisco, and Seattle.

EMERGENCIES Dial **911** for fire, police, and medical emergencies, and ☎ **212/555-9955** for poison control.

HOLIDAYS Government offices, post offices, banks, and many restaurants, stores, and museums are closed on the following national holidays: January 1 (New Year's Day), the third Monday in January (Martin Luther King, Jr. Day), the third Monday in February (Presidents' Day), the last Monday in May (Memorial Day), July 4 (Independence Day), the first Monday in September (Labor Day), the second Monday in October (Columbus Day), November 11 (Veterans Day), the fourth Thursday in November (Thanksgiving Day), and December 25 (Christmas). Election Day is the Tuesday after the first Monday in November.

HOSPITALS   Hospitals convenient to downtown include **Oregon Health & Science University,** 3181 SW Sam Jackson Park Rd. (☎ **503/494-8311;** www.ohsu.edu), **Providence Portland Medical Center,** 4805 NE Glisan St. (☎ **503/574-6595;** http://oregon.providence.org), and **Legacy Good Samaritan,** 1015 NW 22nd Ave. (☎ **503/413-7711;** www.legacyhealth.org). Legacy has a physician referral service at ☎ **503/335-3500.**

INSURANCE   For information on traveler's insurance, trip cancellation insurance, and medical insurance while traveling, please visit www.frommers.com/planning.

INTERNET & WI-FI   Most of Portland's coffee shops offer free Wi-Fi, as do the branches of the **Multnomah County Library** (☎ **503/988-5402;** www.multcolib.org), which also have Internet terminals available to all. Most hotels offer Internet access, though you'll probably have to pay extra.

LEGAL AID   While driving, if you are pulled over for a minor infraction (such as speeding), never attempt to pay the fine directly to a police officer; this could be construed as attempted bribery, a much more serious crime. Pay fines by mail, or directly into the hands of the clerk of the court. If accused of a more serious offense, say and do nothing before consulting a lawyer. In the

U.S., the burden is on the state to prove a person's guilt beyond a reasonable doubt, and everyone has the right to remain silent, whether he or she is suspected of a crime or actually arrested. Once arrested, a person can make one telephone call to a party of his or her choice. The international visitor should call his or her embassy or consulate.

LGBT TRAVELERS   To find out what's going on in the LGBT community, pick up a free copy of the bimonthly *Just Out* (☎ **503/236-1252;** http://blogout.justout.com), or check out the Portland section of http://gaytravel.about.com, written by a local. The **Gay & Lesbian Community Yellow Pages** (☎ **503/230-7701;** www.pdxgayyellowpages.com), available at Powell's City of Books, lists gay-friendly businesses. Also check in with the folks at Portland's **LGBT center** (www.pdxqcenter.org).

MAIL   At press time, domestic postage rates were 29¢ for a postcard and 44¢ for a letter. For international mail, first-class postcards and letters up to 1 ounce cost 98¢ (80¢ to Mexico and Canada). Find more rates and information at www.usps.com. The most convenient downtown post office is **University Station,** 1505 SW 6th Ave. (☎ **800/ASK-USPS** or 503/274-1362; www.usps.com), open Monday through Friday from 7am to 6pm, Saturday from 10am to 3pm.

NEWSPAPERS & MAGAZINES   The *Oregonian* is Portland's major daily newspaper. The *Portland Mercury* and *Willamette Week* are free arts-and-entertainment weeklies.

PASSPORTS   Virtually every air traveler entering the U.S. is required to show a passport.

For Residents of Australia: Call Australian Passport Information Service (☎ **131-232,** or visit www.passports.gov.au).

For **Residents of Canada:** Passport Office, Department of Foreign Affairs and International Trade, Ottawa, ON K1A 0G3 (☎ **800/567-6868;** www.ppt.gc.ca).

For **Residents of Ireland:** Passport Office, Setanta Centre, Molesworth St., Dublin 2 (☎ **01/671-1633;** www.foreignaffairs.gov.ie).

For **Residents of New Zealand:** Passports Office, Department of Internal Affairs, 47 Boulcott St., Wellington, 6011 (☎ **0800/225-050** in New Zealand or 04/474-8100; www.passports.govt.nz).

For **Residents of the United Kingdom:** Visit your nearest passport office, major post office, or travel agency or contact the Identity and Passport Service (IPS), 89 Eccleston Square, London, SW1V 1PN (☎ **0300/222-0000;** www.ips.gov.uk).

PHARMACIES Conveniently located downtown pharmacies include **Rite Aid,** 622 SW Alder St. (☎ **503/226-6791**), which is open 24 hr., and **Central Drug,** 538 SW 4th Ave. (☎ **503/226-2222**). Most large grocery stores have pharmacies as well.

POLICE The **Portland Police Bureau**'s central precinct is at 1111 SW 2nd Ave. (☎ **503/823-0000;** www.portlandpolice.com). Dial **911** for emergencies.

SAFETY Portland is a relatively safe city, but you should take some precautions if you venture into the Chinatown and Old Town districts at night. Don't leave anything valuable in your car while you're hiking in Forest Park. As a general precaution, avoid deserted areas, especially at night, and don't go into public parks at night. Park in well-lit, busy areas whenever possible.

SMOKING Smoking is banned in public indoor spaces throughout the state of Oregon, even bars, as well as within 10 feet of entrances, exits, and windows.

TAXES Oregon is one of only five states with no sales tax, making it a shopper's delight. In Portland, there are 12.5% taxes on both hotel rooms and car rentals (plus an additional fee of 10%–15% if you pick up your rental car at the airport).

TIME Portland is on Pacific time, 3 hours behind the East Coast. In the summer, daylight saving time is observed and clocks are set forward 1 hour.

TIPPING Waiters generally receive 15%–20% of the bill; taxi drivers 15% of fare; bartenders $1 per drink; hotel chamber staff $1–$2 per day; skycaps and valets $1–$2 per bag; and valet parking attendants $1 per ride.

TOILETS Portland may be the only city with its own patented public toilet, the **Portland Loo** (www.portlandloo.com). Find these sleek, solar-powered, 24-hour restrooms along SW Naito Parkway in Waterfront Park at both SW Ash and SW Taylor streets, as well as at NW Glisan Street between SW 5th and 6th avenues, and at Jamison Square at NW Johnson Street and NW 11th Avenue. Some downtown parks have historic comfort stations, including the North Park Blocks.

TRANSIT INFO For 24-hour information on Portland's public transit system, contact **TriMet** at ☎ **503/238-7433** or go to www.trimet.org.

VISAS The U.S. State Department has a **Visa Waiver Program (VWP)** allowing citizens of the following countries to enter the United States without a visa for stays of up to 90 days: Andorra, Australia, Austria, Belgium, Brunei, Czech Republic, Denmark, Estonia, Finland, France, Germany, Greece, Hungary, Iceland, Ireland, Italy, Japan, Latvia, Liechtenstein, Lithuania, Luxembourg, Malta, Monaco, the Netherlands, New

Zealand, Norway, Portugal, San Marino, Singapore, Slovakia, Slovenia, South Korea, Spain, Sweden, Switzerland, and the United Kingdom. (**Note:** This list was accurate at press time; for the most up-to-date list of countries in the VWP, consult http://travel.state.gov/visa.) Even though a visa isn't necessary for citizens of those countries, in an effort to help U.S. officials check travelers against terror watch lists before they arrive at U.S. borders, visitors from VWP countries must register online through the **Electronic System for Travel Authorization (ESTA)** before boarding a plane or a boat to the U.S. Travelers must complete an electronic application providing basic personal and travel eligibility information. The Department of Homeland Security recommends filling out the form at least 3 days before traveling. Authorizations will be valid for up to 2 years or until the traveler's passport expires, whichever comes first. Currently, there is a US$14 fee for the online application. Existing ESTA registrations remain valid through their expiration dates. For more information, go to http://travel.state.gov/visa.

Canadian citizens may enter the United States without visas, but will need to show passports and proof of residence.

Citizens of all other countries must have (1) a valid passport that expires at least 6 months later than the scheduled end of their visit to the U.S.; and (2) a tourist visa.

Portland: **A Brief History**

15,000-13,000 bc Cataclysmic floods carve the Columbia Gorge, with waters reaching as high as Crown Point.

12,300 bc Earliest known human inhabitants in Oregon, near Paisley, 220 miles southeast of Eugene.

1579 English explorer Sir Francis Drake reaches the mouth of the Rogue River in southwest Oregon, turned back by "thicke and stinking fogges."

1792 American captain Robert Gray becomes first to sail into the Columbia River, names it in honor of his ship the *Columbia Rediviva*.

1805 Expedition led by Meriwether Lewis and William Clark reaches the Pacific Ocean at the mouth of the Columbia River, and spends a miserable winter in Fort Clatsop.

1819 Spain cedes all lands above 42 degrees north latitude (California's northern boundary today) to the U.S.

1824 Fort Vancouver, fur-trading outpost of the Hudson's Bay Company, founded across the Columbia River from present-day Portland.

1841 Bartleson-Bidwell Party, the first group to make a wagon crossing of the Oregon Trail, reaches the Willamette Valley from Missouri.

1843 Business partners Asa Lovejoy and William Overton pay 25¢ filing fee to claim 640 acres on the west bank of the Willamette River in present-day Portland; settlers elect provisional government.

1844 Oregon City becomes first incorporated town west of the Rocky Mountains.

1840S-1860S About 400,000 emigrants travel west on the Oregon Trail.

1845 Asa Lovejoy and new partner Francis Pettygrove flip a coin to name the settlement called simply "The Clearing"; Pettygrove wins and names it after his hometown of Portland, Maine.

1848 Oregon becomes first U.S. territory west of the Rockies; Pettygrove sells nearly the entire townsite of Portland to tanner Daniel Lownsdale for $5,000 worth of leather, despite only owning half of it.

1851 City of Portland incorporated.

1853 Horse-powered Stark Street Ferry becomes first to cross the Willamette River.

1879 First telephone lines installed.

1880 First electric street lights arrive.

1883 Northern Pacific Railroad reaches Portland.

1887 First zoo opens in Washington Park.

1888 Steel Bridge #1 opens, the first steel bridge on the West Coast.

1889 Local newspapers call Portland "the most filthy city in the Northern States" with sidewalks that would be a "disgrace to a Russian village."

1905 Lewis and Clark Centennial Exposition held, including the Forestry Building, "the world's greatest log cabin."

1907 Oaks Amusement Park opens; first Rose Festival held.

1908 Portland Police Department hires Lola Greene Baldwin, the nation's first policewoman.

1910 City begins purchasing land that will become Forest Park; first Hawthorne Bridge opens.

1915 Columbia River Gorge scenic highway constructed.

1917 International Rose Test Garden established.

1934 Waterfront strike shuts down shipping in every port on the West Coast for 4 days.

1940S Portland's Kaiser shipyards become the world's leading shipbuilders due to the war effort.

1945 Oregon becomes the only mainland state to suffer civilian war casualties when a Japanese balloon bomb kills a pregnant woman and five children near Bly, Oregon.

1946 Portland State University founded.

1950S Organized crime, corruption, and vice dominate local politics, resulting in indictments of Multnomah county district attorney and Portland's mayor and chief of police.

1957 Elvis Presley performs in front of 14,000 people at Multnomah Stadium (now Jeld-Wen Field), one of the first outdoor stadium rock concerts.

1960S Winemakers plant Oregon's first pinot noir vines in the Umpqua Valley, southwest of Eugene, starting modern era of Oregon winemaking.

1964 Nike founded by University of Oregon track runner Philip Knight and coach Bill Bowerman.

1965 The Beatles play two shows at Memorial Coliseum for 20,000 fans, inspiring Allen Ginsberg's poem "Portland Coliseum."

1971 Classic computer game *The Oregon Trail* introduces history students to dysentery, typhoid, and other hazards of traveling the cross-country pioneer route.

1974 Harbor Drive freeway along downtown waterfront is removed, eventually to be replaced with Waterfront Park.

1977 Portland Trail Blazers win NBA Championship for the first and only time (so far).

1979 City's urban growth boundary established.

1980 Mt. St. Helens erupts, killing 57 people and blanketing Portland in ash.

1985 First light rail train route opens; *Portlandia* statue installed.

1990–91 Northern Spotted Owl listed as threatened under the Endangered Species Act; almost all logging in national forests in northern California, Oregon, and Washington stopped by court order.

1990S Dot-com boom brings an influx of artists, graphic designers, and Internet entrepreneurs to Portland; dot-com bust brings even more from Seattle and San Francisco.

2000S "Jail Blazers" era of the NBA team is marked by fights and charges of sexual assault, drug possession, and dog fighting.

2001 Portland becomes first city in the U.S. to introduce modern streetcar service.

2010 Somali-American student arrested by FBI for plotting to bomb Pioneer Courthouse Square, charged with attempting to use a weapon of mass destruction.

2010 *Portlandia* comedy series premieres on IFC, poking fun at the city "where young people go to retire."

2011 Portland Timbers play their first Major League Soccer game against reigning champions the Colorado Rapids, losing 3–1.

Portland Reads

Portland has long been a magnet for writers and the readers who love them. There's a long list of books by local authors, about Portland, or both. Here are a few classics:

- Jean M. Auel, *The Clan of the Cave Bear*
- Chelsea Cain, *Heartsick*
- Beverly Cleary, *Ramona the Pest*
- Katherine Dunn, *Geek Love*
- Stewart Holbrook, *The Portland Story*
- Ursula K. Le Guin, *The Lathe of Heaven*
- Chuck Palahniuk, *Fugitives and Refugees: A Walk in Portland, Oregon*
- Joe Sacco, *Palestine*

Index

See also Accommodations and Restaurant indexes, below.

Photo **Credits**

p viii: © Ken Cedeno; p 4 top: © Ken Cedeno; p 4 bottom: © Leah Nash / Novus Select; p 5, top: © Leah Nash / Novus Select; p 5 bottom: © Leah Nash / Novus Select; p 6 top: © Leah Nash / Novus Select; p 6 bottom: © Leah Nash / Novus Select; p 7: © Ken Cedeno; p 9: © Ken Cedeno; p 10: © Ken Cedeno; p 11: © Ken Cedeno; p 12: © Ken Cedeno; p 13: © Ken Cedeno; p 15: © Ken Cedeno; p 16, top: © Ken Cedeno; p 16, bottom: © Ken Cedeno; p 17: © Ken Cedeno; p 18, top: © Ken Cedeno; p 18, bottom: © Ken Cedeno; p 19 top: © Leah Nash / Novus Select; p 19, bottom: © Ken Cedeno; p 21: © Leah Nash / Novus Select; p 22 top: © Leah Nash / Novus Select; p 22, bottom: © Leah Nash / Novus Select; p 23: © Leah Nash / Novus Select; p 25: © Ken Cedeno; p 27: © Ken Cedeno; p 28, top: © Ken Cedeno; p 28 bottom: © Ken Cedeno; p 30, top: © Ken Cedeno; p 30, bottom: © Ken Cedeno; p 31: © Leah Nash / Novus Select; p 33: © Leah Nash / Novus Select; p 34: © Ken Cedeno; p 35: © Ken Cedeno; p 36: © Ken Cedeno; p 37: © Leah Nash / Novus Select; p 39: © Ken Cedeno; p 40: © Ken Cedeno; p 41: © Ken Cedeno; p 42, top: © Ken Cedeno; p 42, bottom: © Courtesy Oaks Park Association; p 43: © Ken Cedeno; p 45: © Ken Cedeno; p 46: © Ken Cedeno; p 47: © Ken Cedeno; p 49: © Ken Cedeno; p 50, top: © Ken Cedeno; p 50, bottom: © Ken Cedeno; p 51: © Ken Cedeno; p 52: © Ken Cedeno; p 53: © Ken Cedeno; p 55: © Ken Cedeno; p 56: © Leah Nash / Novus Select; p 57: © Leah Nash / Novus Select; p 59: © Leah Nash / Novus Select; p 60: © Leah Nash / Novus Select; p 61: © Ken Cedeno; p 63: © Ken Cedeno; p 64, top: © Ken Cedeno; p 64, bottom: © Ken Cedeno; p 65: © Ken Cedeno; p 67: © Ken Cedeno; p 68: © Ken Cedeno; p 71 top: © Leah Nash / Novus Select; p 71 bottom: © Leah Nash / Novus Select; p 72 top: © Leah Nash / Novus Select; p 72 bottom: © Leah Nash / Novus Select; p 73: © Leah Nash / Novus Select; p 74: © Ken Cedeno; p 78, top: © Leah Nash / Novus Select; p 78, bottom: © Ken Cedeno; p 79: © Leah Nash / Novus Select; p 80: © Leah Nash / Novus Select; p 81, top: © Ken Cedeno; p 81, bottom: © Ken Cedeno; p 82, top: © Leah Nash / Novus Select; p 82, bottom: © Leah Nash / Novus Select; p 83 top: © Ken Cedeno; p 83 bottom: © Ken Cedeno; p 84: © Leah Nash / Novus Select; p 85: © Leah Nash / Novus Select; p 87: © Leah Nash / Novus Select; p 89, top: © Leah Nash / Novus Select; p 89, bottom: © Leah Nash / Novus Select; p 90: © Ken Cedeno; p 91: © Ken Cedeno; p 93, top: © Leah Nash / Novus Select; p 93, bottom: © Ken Cedeno; p 95: © Ken Cedeno; p 101: © Leah Nash / Novus Select; p 103: © Leah Nash / Novus Select; p 104 top: © Leah Nash / Novus Select; p 104 bottom: © Leah Nash / Novus Select; p 105, top: © Ken Cedeno; p 105 bottom: © Ken Cedeno; p 106: © Leah Nash / Novus Select; p 107, top: © Leah Nash / Novus Select; p 107, bottom: © Leah Nash / Novus Select; p 109: © Leah Nash / Novus Select; p 111: © Leah Nash / Novus Select; p 114: © Leah Nash / Novus Select; p 116 top: © Leah Nash / Novus Select; p 116, bottom: © Leah Nash / Novus Select; p 117: © Ken Cedeno; p 118: © Leah Nash / Novus Select; p 119: © Ken Cedeno; p 120: © Leah Nash / Novus Select; p 121: Leah Nash / Novus Select; p 125: Leah Nash / Novus Select; p 126: Leah Nash / Novus Select; p 127: © Leah Nash / Novus Select; p 128: © Leah Nash / Novus Select; p 129: © Ken Cedeno; p 130: © Courtesy Artists Repertory Theater; p 131: © Ken Cedeno; p 134: © Ken Cedeno; p 136: © Courtesy Hotel Lucia; p 137: © Courtesy Hotel Modera; p 138: © Courtesy Hotel Monaco; p 139: © Brian Robb / Courtesy Mt. Hood Meadows Ski Resort; p 141: © Leah Nash / Novus Select; p 143: © Leah Nash / Novus Select; p 144: © Ken Cedeno; p 145, top: © Leah Nash / Novus Select; p 145, bottom: © Leah Nash / Novus Select; p 147: © Leah Nash / Novus Select; p 149: © Leah Nash / Novus Select; p 150: © Leah Nash / Novus Select; p 151: © Leah Nash / Novus Select; p 153: © Leah Nash / Novus Select; p 154: © Leah Nash / Novus Select; p 155: © Leah Nash, p 156: © Leah Nash / Novus Select; p. 157, top: Leah Nash / Novus Select; p 157, bottom: © Leah Nash / Novus Select; p 158: © Leah Nash / Novus Select; p 159: © Leah Nash / Novus Select

Notes

Notes

Notes